Look What You Made Me Do

A love letter to the fandom era

Kat McKenna

GALLERY YA

I'm your biggest fan, and I can't wait to see who you become.

First published in Great Britain in 2024 by Gallery YA,
an imprint of Simon & Schuster UK Ltd

1 3 5 7 9 10 8 6 4 2

Simon & Schuster UK Ltd
1st Floor, 222 Gray's Inn Road
London WC1X 8HB

Simon & Schuster: Celebrating 100 Years of Publishing in 2024

www.simonandschuster.co.uk
www.simonandschuster.com.au
www.simonandschuster.co.in

Simon & Schuster Australia, Sydney
Simon & Schuster India, New Delhi

A CIP catalogue record for this book is available from the British Library.

PB ISBN 978-1-3985-3280-9
eBook ISBN 978-1-3985-3282-3
eAudio ISBN 978-1-3985-3281-6

MIX
Paper | Supporting
responsible forestry
FSC® C023419

FOREWORD

In the words of a woman I admire very much, 'I think it's important that you know that I will never change, but I'll never stay the same either.'

The subject of this book, one Taylor Alison Swift, is the most inspiring woman I know. She's also the fastest-moving woman I know. Therefore, the content of this book, while maintaining a culturally and critically current representation of Taylor, may not cover every facet of her life to date – whether that be unexpected album drops, handsome American football players, secret collaborations, or . . . who knows?!

This is part of what makes it so exciting to be a Taylor Swift fan. We can always expect surprises.

Additionally, the social media landscape at the time of writing is ever-changing, including trends, platform names, tensions, and political alliances. I have tried to ensure that all references and named platforms are at the very least historically accurate to the time featured. I hope you'll fill in the gaps for me if anything has shifted dramatically by the time this book is in your hands. Thank you for choosing to read it.

CONTENTS

TODAY WAS A FAIRYTALE

'Just be yourself.
There is no-one better.'
— TAYLOR SWIFT

'I just wanted to listen to
Taylor Swift alone.'
— JESS DAY, *NEW GIRL*

This is not a book about Taylor Swift. This is a book about *you*. About me. About us.

This book is for the fans.

I've been a fan of things for as long as I can remember. But I don't think I have ever profoundly cared about something as much as I care about Taylor Swift.

I remember exactly where I was when I first heard a Taylor Swift song. It was February 2010, and a close friend and I had gone to the cinema to celebrate her birthday. We had an annual tradition – she would pick the cheesiest romcom that we would enjoy together. We'd survived *Bride Wars*, *27 Dresses*, *He's Just Not That Into You* – by now cult classics, comfort films that don't get made to the same (slightly problematic) standard anymore. In 2010, my dear friend's pick was *Valentine's Day* – one of those popular-at-the-time multi-plot movies, starring abundant A-listers such as Bradley Cooper, Katherine Heigl . . . and Taylor Swift.

I actually loved the film. As the final scenes played out satisfyingly, a song I had never heard before accompanied them. The first introductory plucks of the guitar strings and smart, sweet lyrics filled the cinema. I nudged my friend and asked, 'What is this? Is this Taylor Swift?'

I had, of course, heard of Taylor. As a diehard pop music fan I'd gone through the cycles of being mocked endlessly for loving Girls Aloud, McFly and other artists that might appeal to young people but who rarely receive credibility beyond their fanbase or teenagers. Taylor Swift was, at the time, largely known by the world for the men she dated, not her music. I had no doubt made the same judgement as others, dismissing her as gossip fodder.

Swift starred in *Valentine's Day*, art imitating life as she played a high-school beauty dating Taylor Lautner (her real-life boyfriend at the time). I was surprised by her instant likeability and her – still developing – acting skills. I had a good chance of guessing the artist performing the song that filled the cinema. And I was completely disarmed to find how much I loved it.

When I heard 'Today Was a Fairytale', my life changed. That is not an overstatement. Since then, Taylor Swift has been with me on my life's journey.

A confidante, an inspiration and an escape from reality, Taylor is more than just music to me,

though her genius lyrics and incredible artistry is what drew me in, and sits at the centre of my continued dedication. The imbalance in our relationship doesn't matter – I know her, and I feel that, through her artistry, she sees me. More than that, she has helped me feel seen.

After the film, I pored over Taylor's back catalogue: in 2010, that was *Speak Now*, *Fearless* and *Debut*. I couldn't believe what I had stumbled upon – a treasure trove of perfect pop country music but, more importantly, a wordsmith who it seemed could see into my soul, could articulate how I felt about experiences that had previously seemed unique to me, *my* life, *my* feelings. I have always made only one judgement upon music – if the lyricism is strong, if the songs can move me with words, count me in.

But this was more than that. This was an artist whose technically excellent music (especially looking back now, knowing she was between eighteen and twenty-one years old at the time of writing those albums) opened up my eyes, my mind and my heart.

So I became a passionate and dedicated Taylor Swift advocate, telling anyone who would listen that she was actually a lyrical genius, hugely misunderstood by the media. People needed to know that she was a talented and smart musician who wrote her own songs and played her own instruments. The injustice that she was being portrayed as little more than a 'maneater' was something I felt personally. Her instant relatability and brutally honest portrayal of the feelings of young women like me was something we needed in the world, something I had never known.

It might be hard reading this, to imagine that there was ever a time when Taylor Swift was not universally loved, respected and idolised. But there is a day I remember all too well. During a conversation with my colleagues I compared Taylor Swift to Adele, another blessing of a talented woman in the music industry. Her first album, 19, was released in 2008, and Adele took the UK charts by storm – heralded as a raw, incredible talent who had an unparalleled ability to express the emotions of love and heartbreak that we all felt. She did so beautifully, in the form of incredible lyrics and thoughtful balladic hits – and was instantly critically acclaimed and approved by more serious music journalists, outlets and fans.

Aha, I thought to myself – *that's* exactly *what Taylor Swift does!* Admittedly, at this point in time, she didn't have the same accolades or advocates in music journalism. I shared this viewpoint with my peers, and was left embarrassed. I had read the room wrong. Don't be *ridiculous*, they all said. Adele is a *real* artist. She's a *songwriter*. A *genius*.

So is Taylor! I cried – vindicated, excited to share, to bring my friends a new artist to love.

But I was told in no uncertain terms, for the first time and certainly not for the last time, that I was wrong: Taylor Swift is NOT the same as Adele. She's young, she's naive, she just dates boys and writes about them for her revenge. She's not even that talented, and she certainly isn't on the same level as Adele.

Now of course this is no fault of Adele's, or my peers at

'She put my thoughts and feelings into coherent, beautiful words.

She expressed my feelings for me in a way I couldn't.'

that time. The perception of pop music – and particularly that of young female artists – is that the music loved by young girls was (and still is) not considered interesting or relevant to most of society. The thoughts and feelings of women are not important, and we certainly shouldn't have to hear them document every step of their heartbreak. If this young woman insists on publicly dating all these famous, equally vapid – but rarely criticised – men, then that's her problem. Why do we have to hear about it? What point of view did Taylor Swift have that *actually mattered*?

It didn't seem to matter that while Taylor Swift's writing style was inspired by her life, those experiences she was having, I was having too. Discrediting her experiences was to indirectly discredit the feelings I had about mine.

So, I kept Taylor as a closely guarded secret for myself. Looking back now, perhaps this is why I held her so close to my heart. My fandom deepened into more than just liking her songs, thinking she was pretty, or marvelling over her transparency about dating A-listers such as Harry Styles, John Mayer and Jake Gyllenhaal. Taylor Swift said things in her songs that I, as a young adult, had never heard before. She put my thoughts and feelings into coherent, beautiful words. She expressed my feelings for me in a way I couldn't. Now, in my thirties, I can honestly say that Taylor's music has helped me process emotional responses to everything from the heartbreak of parental divorce, the pain of trying too hard and pangs of unrequited love.

Taylor, as she and I grew up in tandem, started to publicly challenge and dismiss the concept of being 'just' a woman. Watching her grow in confidence, cutting off suggestive interviews with reporters about her love life, helped me build my own feminism, my own burgeoning frustrations about living in a world made for men. A scene in her Netflix documentary, *Miss Americana*, sees Taylor apologising for talking about her personal journey with reconstructing feminism. She catches herself, and comments wryly, 'Sorry, was I loud? In my own house that I bought, with the songs that I wrote, about my own life?' If I ever need a personal reminder that I'm enough, or not 'too much', I come back to that clip.

I have always been a person with the disposition to be a fan. I had almost no friends as a child. I was deeply shy and struggled through the early stages of adolescence. I found my first sense of belonging as a teen in online chat rooms discussing *Buffy The Vampire Slayer* with strangers who became friends, with blinking avatars who became writing partners, and even one who became my first love. I don't think I understood then the deep sense of belonging that being a fan can bring you, the community it can gift you

'I don't think
I understood then
the deep sense
of belonging
that being a fan
can bring you,
the community it
can gift you through
shared experiences
and passions.'

through shared experiences and passions. When I find something or someone that speaks to me, I latch on. That's just who I am.

I moved through *Buffy* chatrooms into *Harry Potter*. Back in simpler times, when the creator of Potter was a warm voice in our minds and not a wielder of problematic messages online, I was OBSESSED. I read *Harry Potter and the Philosopher's Stone* as a young teen – what followed was years of dedicated, intricate love of everything about those books. It also led me into the world of fanfiction. I had been a wannabe author for as long as I could remember; my mum a deeply creative writer who is still often found living in the stories in her head. I followed suit, escaping into alternative versions of worlds I knew inside out.

Books had been my comfort and escape as a young, shy child living in an unhappy home. Fanfiction became another place to disappear, to reimagine a familiar world a thousand times over, and as I grew into adolescence and started experiencing my own versions of young love and lust, I could create romances between the characters I 'shipped' intensely. Shipping, the desire for two characters or people to be romantically linked, is a commonly featured part of being in fandom culture – a fantasy with the escapism.

As adulthood emerged, the escapism took second string. I did the things that someone growing up does. I moved out of the family home and went to university. I bagged my first job in London. I dated, I fell in love, I went out with friends, I built my career. Fandom fell away.

It is time consuming, a full-time job, to be a good fan. It takes single-minded focus and, back then, hours spent on computers blocking the phone line with dial-up internet. Now our smartphones help us consume the world instantly, with no data limit to burden us.

Life took over, but I always held my fandom close to my heart. Fandom truly helped me become who I was, and I will always be grateful that the people I knew then – and the stories and characters and worlds I loved so deeply that gave me the strength to get through hard times – helped me form into the person who found the confidence to be me.

So, how does Taylor Swift fit into my life now? Am I a Swiftie, a superfan, a stan? The answer is yes . . . and no. As I have moved through a career in which social media, digital platforms and fan marketing have played a prominent role, my analytical brain can see both sides of the coin. I have been lucky enough to work with celebrities and even get to know a couple of them on a deeper level. I've learned that all is never as it seems, and behind every household name is a person – as well as an army of staff who are there to smooth over the cracks, to unruffle the creases and to hide the disasters.

I am a fan, but I am also a critic. I have spent years fascinated by the world of celebrity, examining the depths and complexities of fan life. What do fans get from kinships with stars? When does loyalty turn to resentment?

Let's travel together through the world of fandom: the reasons we become fans, the first fans, the minds of fans. We'll explore parasocial relationships and stans, fan hierarchies and the wide range of fandoms that exist – even looking at some of the more niche communities that are growing bigger as algorithms make it easier to find our tribes. We'll examine how artists such as Taylor empower their fans and followers, how celebrities sharing their experiences, politics and worlds can both inspire and isolate.

It is important as well to understand the wider world of celebrity. There are platforms that boost, build or break down the careers of some of the world's biggest stars – gossip podcasts and blind items, superfans on TikTok, and troll sites. What about cancel culture – is it okay to hold our idols accountable? As we sit squarely in the age of Gen-Z and the new, younger Alpha generation, are the stars we choose to celebrate and the accountability we demand a step towards the end of toxic celebrities?

With cancel culture, we are starting to see the emergence of an anti-celebrity culture in some stars – frontmen like Matty Healy of The 1975 and

Yungblud display an almost humorous annoyance with the notion of fame, preferring to dedicate themselves only to their art and their fans. Can our starlets of the twenty-first century sustain their fanbases, and indeed their careers, if they don't lean into the rocky world of fan culture? On the other path, what about 'unproblematic' stars like Harry Styles – those who seem to soar through the tests and challenges of online fan culture. How do they do it?

And why has Taylor Swift in particular impacted us more than other stars? Taylor is the most famous she has ever been, and as a fan who has watched her rise from country-music teen hopeful to sequin-adorned idol selling out stadiums worldwide, there has never been a better time to ask how she got there – and how her fans helped. Her fans, her fame and the world Swift has built for herself and for us is the most fascinating out there today.

CHAPTER 1

LOVE STORY

The First Fans

Let's step back in time. Us Swifties are not the first fans. That's right; before you and I binge-watched Easter-egg theories and hand-beaded friendship bracelets, there was already a whole world of fandom to set the scene for us.

It is human nature to love, and it is human nature to find community.

We all love to love stuff, whether that be music, food, graphic novels or book characters. We even love love itself. There are whole fandoms based around rooting for favourite imaginary couples, or superstars who have only to be photographed together once to set our imaginations alight. More so, we *love* to let people *know* we love stuff.

That hasn't changed in thousands of years. The difference is that now we can talk to anyone about what we love – anywhere across the world, at any time of day or night, without leaving our sofa (from one introvert to another: *yay*).

Fandom has been around for as long as there has been something to admire, desire or aspire to – and long before we got our iPhones. Look at the ruins of the Colosseum in Rome, still standing in awe-inspiring visibility to remind us of the revered Gladiators of 80AD and their infamous fights and showmanship. Romans would visit the looming, unbelievably stunning site in their swarms to cheer on the bloodthirsty fights of men they came to worship. It didn't matter if that fight was against beast or fellow man – the people wanted to be entertained, and so entertainment is what they got.

There was even tiered seating in the Colosseum, mirroring the experiences of fans today who go out of their way to see stars in arenas and stadiums no matter how far away or tiny their starlet may look. The term 'nosebleed seats' has been around since the 1950s to describe the altitude of visitors to football stadiums – but it is possible to imagine that the Ancient Romans were also complaining about terrible views and limited seating, though possibly only to their closest mates (what did they do without Reddit?!). Today, the battle isn't with our fellow man on a dirt floor in front of the masses – it's via sites like Ticketmaster or anonymous forums and 'X' threads, all of us desperately trying to be better fans than each other.

As the ability to communicate more broadly across the globe has increased, so has the concept of fandom. Seemingly directly related to our sense of self, fandom is now a core part of celebrity culture – we simply do not exist without the things and people we love (and hate) beyond measure. In Sean Redmond's academic text on all things fame, *Celebrity*, he posits that:

> *'People get their identities through both how they see themselves and how they are seen by others . . . stars and celebrities offer people particularly appealing identity positions that they are asked to "take up".'*

We can see why fandom is not only appealing, but consistently growing, as we search for identity in an ever-noisier world. The abundance of artists, content and material possessions has never been so saturated – and our access to the upper echelons through social media has never made it feel so intimate and engaging.

Our sense of self has been challenged in recent years by the Coronavirus pandemic. Seeking comfort online was a growing norm in the late 2010s, but being locked in our homes, experiencing an increasing and rapid fear of the outside world gave us even more rational reason to trust our phones more than our friends; to find solace on screen rather than in social settings. It's no surprise that fandom communities are, at present, more passionate and prominent than they have ever been.

Before that, though, as with Ancient Rome, there were simpler times. The meaning of 'fandom' and being a fan has developed in society as organically as the notion of celebrity itself – but where did it all begin?

Whenever a celebrity rises from bright spark to megastar we can see patterns. By being different, being *fearless*, and giving us something we have never seen before (but perhaps imagined or hoped to have ourselves) that bright spark creates a seed that takes root, germinates and grows . . . in this case into a superstar. And to have fans, we need stars.

If we are looking to public figures to help formulate our own sense of identity, then seeing that reflected back at us by the shiniest stars is an empowering and awe-inspiring concept that can foster lifelong loyalty. We want to feel like the people who have made it, and we want them to know us. After all, they were once just like us.

Back in the 1950s, Elvis Presley launched his music career in the US market, heavily inspired by African-American music. Over the next ten years, Elvis rocketed to stardom on the wave of legions of obsessed, adoring fans who were seeing something for the first time.

Known then and now as the King, Elvis is regarded as one of the most significant figures in music of the twentieth century. How did he find his way to this position of cultural royalty? It's unarguable that Elvis's fanbase was, at the height of his fame, vast, dedicated, passionate – and a little bit in love. Drawn in by a unique voice, musical experimentation and a never-seen-before image – from the slicked curl in his hair to alluringly tight-fitting leather jumpsuits – Elvis gave people something to talk about, and somebody to love. His image was backed up by a long-established love of music; he was gifted his first guitar at ten years old, despite growing up in poverty. A young man from humble beginnings, Elvis went on to make hits that are still played, loved and cited as inspiration by musicians today.

The hysteria of the Elvis fanbase built as his own celebrity identity formed and grew. Nothing like it had ever been witnessed before. Seen as a white man performing and celebrating traditionally Black ideals of blues and rock music, Elvis was a risktaker and a rulebreaker. And don't we all love a bad boy?

Fandom is about more than girls having hysterical crushes on famous men. It must be acknowledged that Elvis was set apart not only by his music, but also by his rebellious, romantic look. Possibly the first thing you think of when you imagine Elvis is him wearing an all-leather boilersuit, rocking his hips to 'Jailhouse Rock'. Yup, Elvis was a hottie and he gave fans something to talk about beyond the music.

Elvis's iconic and world-first 1973 *Aloha From Hawaii*

show was the first-ever musical performance to be streamed in colour – to over forty countries and a record-breaking 1.5 billion fans. The show was viewed by more than *double* the number of people who watched the moon landing. Elvis was officially more famous than space.

Hot on the heels of Presley, across the pond, four young men in their late teens from Liverpool offered another classic example of how fresh, unique takes in artistry and aesthetics can catapult unknowns into timeless, historical fame. The Beatles – John, Paul, George and Ringo – remain to this day the yardstick upon which most musical records are based, led into the limelight by a legion of mostly female fans.

The Beatles' fanbase is largely remembered and recognised to have been full of screaming young girls. As Hannah Ewan observes in her book inspired by the One Direction fandom, *Fangirls*, 'Suddenly fans weren't just part of something bigger than themselves . . . they were as important as the artists they loved. The words "Beatle mania" were stamped on headlines, and if you were part of this "madness" . . . the spotlight was on you.' With the rise of television and aired news and concerts, The Beatles marked a first-time media focus on the fanbase. Now everyone could see the true dedication. These screaming, hysterical fans were seen as just that – out of their minds.

Eventually their fanbase widened out to people with more 'credible' taste in music – and so four global superstars were born. Guys, I think I've seen this film before . . .

Both The Beatles and Elvis came from modest backgrounds, working tirelessly to achieve their dreams and represent 'real people'. For John, Paul, Ringo and George to succeed, they had to do so against the odds. They didn't have access to money, to industry incircles – they were just like us. This 'just like us' philosophy has gone on to sit at the heart of many celebrity stories, as well as multi-million-pound global television franchises like *Big Brother*, *Pop Idol* and *The X Factor* – franchises that take everyday nobodies with a spectacular talent and ask the audience to choose their winner.

As the media played a bigger role in influencing us, it made celebrities – and their fans – more of a focus in everyday society. And so we started to see fame get bigger too.

With the rise of the press and clickbait headlines, there was more space than ever for young people to discover music, and as such, discover the artists that created it. Alongside these discoveries came more access to the private, personal lives of celebs. It also showed us how to be a fan. The media provided keen young generations with a 'how to', an instructional guide for budding fans to follow: if you love your artist enough, you'll show it like these fans do. You have permission to be more hysterical, more dedicated, more fanatical than the last girl you met who loved The Beatles, or One Direction, or Taylor Swift. If these people I see on my television are standing outside hotel rooms, or sleeping outside venues to get the best spot, then so must I.

We can see these patterns mirrored and amplified in today's fandom – where TV brought the likes of Elvis, The Beatles and David Bowie into the moving image, now we have social media to help us get to know our idols even better. We can see what they eat for breakfast, what they're listening to, where they're hanging out – even lyrics that hint at the street they once lived on, such as those from Taylor Swift's much-loved 'Cornelia Street'.

These locations can become places of worship for fans – amplified by the constant access we have, the live location updates and the ease with which we can collect fellow fans to stand together in patronage to these spots and the noteworthy moments that occured there. In 2023 fans flocked to Cornelia Street to lay flowers to mourn the end of Taylor Swift's six-year relationship with Joe Alwyn.

It doesn't matter that Swift hasn't lived on Cornelia Street for years, and fans of course do not have a full insight into the relationship between her and Alwyn (only what she writes in her songs from her point of view, or glimpses from paparazzi photos, gossip pages and social media). However, the strong pull to mark, or even honour or mourn, such a monumental relationship in Swift's life clearly moves fans enough to need to inhabit the same physical space she once did, no matter how briefly.

*

You'd have to be living on another planet not to have heard of or witnessed the impact of David Bowie. Bowie was revered in the 1970s, '80s and '90s by journalists, rock stars and young people around the world'. Bowie was also a hypnotic, powerful representative for young men, particularly the queer community, expanding his artistry into politics. Bowie was a heartthrob with great provocation, but his particular brand of stardom and sexuality was a huge statement – he was far more intentional about expressing his unique artistry and political position than other musical performers who came before him.

David Bowie was one of the first artists to showcase notions of 'eras' and identity, known famously to be a shapeshifter through his career. Bowie kept fans, critics and music lovers alike on their toes via his stints as characters such Ziggy Stardust, Aladdin Sane and the Thin White Duke. Every era of Bowie's career created more conversation, and surely made him braver and bolder. He courted fascination by leaving people wanting more and wondering what was next. Through imitation and fashion choices his fans aspired to be just like him – and whichever character he presented at each particular time.

We can see this happening today with Lady Gaga, Beyoncé and, of course, Taylor Swift.

Bowie's artistry took inspiration from high art, faraway continents, alien cultures and a strong creative mind.

Today, celebrities have access to astronomical budgets and high-couture designers with vast creative flair to help them form their next media-worthy look. But it still captures our imagination, our attention and tells a story that we totally buy into.

Media power, pop idols and the social network

In the Channel 4 documentary, *Crazy About One Direction*, it is suggested that 1D were the first band to truly benefit from social media buzz. At the time of their formation on *The X Factor*, marketing teams behind the scenes had a clear strategy: the rise of 'X' was impacting how singers became stars. Studying the optics of each band member or solo act on the platform, weekly reports were created to help the producers at ITV, and the hitmakers at Simon Cowell's production company SyCo, understand the levels of popularity around each live show in a way that no act had ever done before. Hashtags were charted, mentions were documented, and follower counts were watched like a hawk. ITV could present all five boys in the band on social media – with 'X' accounts ready to go before they reached any level of fame – and test the public interest.

Harry, Liam, Louis, Niall and Zayn all had astronomical 'X' followings by the time *The X Factor* season 7 final aired in December 2010. They also had something else – an army of teenage girls ready to fall in love with them, to go into bat for them, and to go to any measures for a chance to know them better – even to meet them.

Crazy About One Direction shows us the most passionate examples of fandom. We see girls who are spotlighted as superfans, emotional, starry eyed and limitless. In one lengthy portion of the documentary, fans use social media to discover which hotel the band is staying in, going to all measures to meet their beloveds. 'X' is as responsible for the heartbreak as it is the highs: one scene portrays the girls devastated to learn that the band have tweeted that they are on their way to the next performance city – making their hunt for personal contact futile.

The show has been criticized by superfans but it is truly an uncomfortably honest look at just how far fans might go, and how much their favourite artists mean to them. The personal connection that fans felt towards One Direction was amplified by the closeness they felt through being part of their journey from normal lads to overnight stars, and through the literal presence of the boys in their phones, in their pockets – or on their laptops – in their bedrooms. You didn't have to leave home to connect with the band, though if you did, did that make you more connected? When passion is faced with passion, who wins the battle of being the 'best fan'?

Social media is today's black-and-white performance of 'Jailhouse Rock'. It is the *Aloha from Hawaii* show, but made accessible daily – anytime you want, anywhere you want. Streaming a performance in the 1970s to billions of fans was an unheard of phenomenon – today, we can whip out our phones, open TikTok and watch concert moments in high definition whenever we want. The Beatles and their headlines feel like a distant dream, whereas now we see fan-created reporting on TikTok the minute something remotely newsworthy happens.

As for Bowie and his radical dress sense, we can now find out exactly which pumps or oversized white shirt Taylor Swift wore within hours, simply by looking at our favourite Instagram account documenting every stitch of clothing, or being fed adverts by keen fashion brands showcasing celebrities wearing their items. And we can buy and wear them ourselves to be just like her.

'As we get deeper into a world where there are hardly any limits, where does our **fandom start**, and when should our access to celebrity STOP?'

Where do the boundaries lie? As we get deeper into a world where there are hardly any limits, where does our fandom start, and when should our access to celebrity stop? Is the new way of loving things having an effect on our sense of fandom? Is it easier to be a superfan now that we can all tell each other how much we love stuff, and what to love, online? What kinds of people today are driven towards such dedication?

Who *are* the fans? What draws us in, what drives us? If celebrity privacy and artistry only lasts as long as the gap between today and tomorrow's Instagram stories, how do we keep mystery alive?

CHAPTER 2

GIRL AT HOME

What is a Fan?

fan *(noun)*: a person who admires somebody/something or enjoys watching or listening to somebody/something very much

Oxford English Dictionary

Fans have existed for centuries. We know the basics of who fans are as set out opposite by the Oxford English Dictionary definition – a person who loves something, usually in the public eye, and often with an element of experience involved, be that of sports games, movies and television shows or musical entertainment.

Over the years, though, With the invention of the internet, gone are the days of loving that special someone or something in isolation – if you want to reach out to likeminded people, there are increasingly more and more ways that can be done.

Online communities have been around since as early as the 1990s. From online communities we build fandoms. Sherry Turkle, in *Clicking In* (edited by Lynn Hershman Leeson), describes these online communities as 'social virtual realities'. Of course, online communities have come a long way since 1996, and we are seeing more than ever that our digital reality and our offline realities are almost completely merged. Young people today do not need to make the distinction because they can take their online friends and foes with them everywhere. Mobile phones and the internet have undoubtedly changed fan culture forever.

Fandoms fascinate academics – with experts dedicating their careers to trying to figure out just what causes fans to behave the way they do: what makes us tick, what pisses us off and what sends us crazy with excitement.

Henry Jenkins is one of those academics. He has extensively researched online communities and subcultures, writing about fanfiction, fan communities and the patterns that exist within them. He talks about 'self-organised groups' – and when we take a step back from ourselves, we can see this is an important observation. In every other element of life we are handed our friends. We don't get to vet our classmates before we start at a new school. But if we join a club or a fandom, we are self-selecting the tribe of people we want to be connected to. This is very cool, and unlike many other connections we make in life.

Jenkins also observes that:

'the speed and frequency of communication may intensify the social bonds within the fan community . . . fans may interact daily, if not hourly, online. Geographically isolated fans can feel much more connected to the fan community and home ridden fans enjoy a new level of acceptance.'

Again, super cool. Fandom isolates nobody, and accepts anybody who shares a like or love. Some of the best friendships can be made simply by connecting with others over a love of something and communicating about it. As I have mentioned, as humans we crave connection. If we can't always find it in traditional settings, fandom opens a way to

'Fandom isolates nobody, and accepts anybody who shares a like or love.'

find yourself. This is part of my story, and I have no doubt it is part of yours too.

When I was in fandom, in the early 2000s, there was one big difference. There was a secretive nature to the fan communities I inhabited. Most people used pseudonyms online to engage in fandoms, and it wasn't perceived as an aspirational thing to be passionately enthusiastic about something outside of 'real life'. There was a line between our everyday lives and the things we consumed.

That's not to say that my dedication to fandom was anything less than all in. In a life where I was limited in my friendships, awkward in my adolescence and deeply uncool, having communities online was the one thing I had to be excited about every day. It was my escape from reality, and I held it close to my heart.

If you'd told me then that fandom would become widespread, mainstream and even aspirational just a few years later, I think that would have made teen me very happy.

Making fandom cool

There is something of a reclamation of fandom happening with today's generation of young people. Online cultures and growing fan spaces have meant that so many people have found their tribe, and those tribes are helping to define what everybody else consumes. Adding power to fandom is to add relevance and interest from outside – if being in a fandom makes you an influencer, a tastemaker, then being in fandoms makes you cool.

Rainbow Rowell's bestselling novel *Fangirl* is one of the most accurate fictional depictions of being a fan that I have read. *Fangirl* shows us twin sisters Cath and Wren as they embark on their first year at university and navigate life in a new environment amidst personal challenges. Cath is a prolific and highly revered online fanfiction writer in the imagined Simon Snow universe. Cath writes fanfiction read by thousands of fans online and is forced to balance and understand her fandom life alongside her real-world life as it becomes increasingly hard to escape from.

Fangirl invited a world of previously unseen fangirls to feel represented in the pages of Rowell's book – you could even read Cath's fanfiction as part of the text. Rainbow Rowell did something so incredibly insightful with those stories within the story – if you looked closely enough, you could see how Cath's own experiences and learnings came through in the world of her fanfiction stars, Simon and Baz. For those who write it, fanfiction can be a therapeutic way of unpacking your own curiosities, life challenges and romantic leanings. *Fangirl* explores this beautifully, and helped many a fan feel validated and seen.

At Rainbow Rowell's first UK book events (which I was

very lucky to attend and help plan as part of my job at the time), I will always remember the audience. They were passionate, adoring fans. Yes, of course they were fans of books and of Rainbow, but they were also fans of other things. There were Whovians, Potterheads and Johnlock connoisseurs – all finally feeling represented in popular fiction. Slash fanfiction (the art of writing same-sex, often male/male romance) or 'shipping' can feel like a very private experience, often a way to explore feelings of love and lust, gender identity and sexuality . . . or just get some serious young adulthood feels out of your system. These romantic stories, featuring characters you can envisage inside out, helped me as a young adult to understand many confusing things about my own life. It's not so different from reading *Twilight* or watching *Never Have I Ever* – we all have tools in life to help us understand what we're going through, particularly when we're young and experiencing so much for the very first time.

Rowell's fans struck me – as they sat down, row by row, and patiently waited in line to meet the author who had expressed their own community so well – as a mirror of myself as a teen. I looked at them, and they looked past me to their beloved author, and in them I remembered that feeling of community, that sense of self-discovery. I too had been an awkward, painfully shy, private but proud fanfiction reader and writer; an avid and obsessive fangirl of many things. Every few years I'd move from one beloved show or story to another, pouring myself into every element of every glorious episode or chapter or book or series.

But it was my biggest kept secret – something I never spoke about even as I grew up and out of fandom. Fifteen years ago, it *wasn't* cool to be a fan. It was considered kind of weird. So I had found my tribe, the first group of people I had known who had ever made me feel funny or cool or interesting, and those people existed online. We imagined new worlds, we reimagined our favourite ones, and we shared something: we all loved the same thing. I learned that I was talented at Photoshop by making fan art. The first writing I ever did was *Harry Potter* fanfiction. I learned skills, I found acceptance, and I never shared it with a single person outside of my slow, whirring old laptop.

What we see today is amazing, in my opinion. A plethora of young people online are excited to be passionate about the thing, person or story they love the most. There is no shame or secrets.

Fans validate one another in their fandom by simply sharing it – not only in spirit, but in memes, in tweets, in WhatsApp groups that are dedicated to your idol. And the more we share it, the more celebrities take notice. They are becoming part of our fandom too.

Taking back the narrative

Have you heard of 'the fourth wall'? You might not, as it feels we are a long way on from its heyday. The fourth wall refers to the invisible barrier that is drawn between performer and fan. When that wall – strategically placed in front of us when it was useful to the narrative – started falling down more frequently, due to the rise of social media and hourly access to celebrities, so did fandom.

There is often more to being a fan than just loving something, especially in the world of fandom today. It is now totally possible to get to know our favourite movie stars, musicians and influencers on an hourly basis, and especially with the rise of no-limit, high-frequency apps such as Instagram and Instagram Stories, and TikTok, we have more access than we've ever had to each other.

There is perhaps some positive to losing the fourth wall in favour of celebrities and their associates firing off Stories and subtweets. We so often hear the phrase 'taking back the narrative' or 'reclaiming my truth'. The reality is that this has been a hard-fought luxury, and is still a navigational challenge today. Strategic messaging and being an 'open book' is very much a choice attached with risks for a celebrity – but there are some, like Paris Hilton, Britney Spears and Katie Price, who find it liberating, finally able to (as far as we can tell) 100 per cent control their narrative on social media after years of being hunted by the media and paparazzi.

This does two things: it blurs the lines between friend and famous, and it makes it feel as though we have as much access to celebrities as we do our everyday companions. It also means that celebrities have access to us, if they want it. The ability for singers, showrunners and story makers to communicate with fans blurs the lines even further, and challenges the boundaries that are in place in the celebrity world.

Taylor Swift takes this one step further – she has not just taken back her narrative, she is now at a point where she is, seemingly, in full control of the messaging she puts out. How she does this? Through her lyrics, yes, but also through her fanbase – who are loyal, listening, and ready to make that messaging into lore. And who can argue with lore?

Are you ready for it?

Taylor Swift is one of a kind. She is a talent very much of the generation and industry landscape she was built up into – one that was fighting with a move to digital listening platforms, streaming services and music piracy. Her authentic and honest, impulsive and human approach to her presence in the music industry leads her to be talked about frequently. Her music is not only brilliant – filling a much-needed gap in the market for younger generations – it is also honest, compassionate and diary-like. It is no surprise that Taylor has collected an army of loyal Swifties, as her fanbase is known.

The Swifties tell us everything we know and more about fandom. They are a united front, and yet divided and hierarchical. They exist in generations, or Eras, with each offering a different way to be a 'good' and 'proper' fan. They love music, and they love Taylor. Some *only* love Taylor's music. Swifties are usually invested in her personal life, and would do almost anything to help boost her professional success. They will spend money, adorn themselves in merchandise and friendship bracelets at live shows, and even rebuy Taylor's music as it is being re-recorded, in order for her to take back ownership of it. Her fans will follow Easter eggs passionately, don detective gear proudly, and help each other to uncover what's coming next in the Taylor Swift multiverse. They will happily educate the lesser-informed followers and fans. They jump from platform to platform on social media and dominate it.

We can learn so much from Taylor's fandom – which so often seems to go where no fanbase has gone before. They set tones, trends, social media etiquette and rules, and they tell us so much about the nature of life as a fan. Their unique relationship with their idol is both parasocial and personal. Sometimes . . . they go way too far. There has never been a more empowering time to be a fan, and there has never been a more interesting fandom than Taylor Swift's.

CHAPTER 3

MISS AMERICANA

Who's Taylor Swift, Anyway?

Taylor Alison Swift was born on 13 December 1989 in Pennsylvania, USA. She has a brother, Austin, and her parents Alison and Scott were both career-driven successful people. Supportive of their children, Taylor Swift's upbringing – on a Christmas tree farm, no less! – was musical from an early age.

Taylor began writing songs from eleven years old, inspired by country music stars such as the Dixie Chicks, Shania Twain and LeAnn Rimes. A *Guardian* interview from 2012 states, '[Swift] reminisces about the Shania Twain songs from her childhood "that could make you want to just run around the block four times and daydream about everything".' Swift is known for lyrics full of honesty and feeling, similar to Shania Twain's early work, but they possess a sense of escapism, fantasy and whimsy, too, notably , notably in her earlier work but also later albums such as *folklore* and *evermore*.

As a young girl, Swift was also inspired by her maternal grandmother, a successful opera singer, who died in 2003. Swift honours her grandmother's spirit and talent in the *evermore* track, 'marjorie', and it is clear how deeply she holds that spirit and creativity as an inspiration. She even included the song in her 2023 Eras Tour setlist, honouring Marjorie's memory by including her voice in the backing track of the performance. She talks at length in an interview with Zane Lowe about her sadness and regret at not having had an opportunity to get to know her better.

It is this openness, the combination of vulnerability and towering strength, that frames Taylor Swift as a rare gem in the entertainment industry. Her rising fame has never faltered her ability to be human with her audience, remaining the same, likeable and almost childlike spirit that she was at the beginning of her career. Taylor Swift remains everybody's friend. At the opening of all her live shows, she announces enthusiastically with a charming smile, 'Hi, I'm Taylor!' – as if we didn't all already know. Yet she has reached highly aspirational levels of celebrity, possessing an 'X-factor' aura which only shines brighter as her fame accelerates.

Taylor's parents agreed to make a move from Pennsylvania to Nashville, at her request, at just fourteen years old, to help her pursue a career in music. Country music was the young Taylor Swift's focus, and Nashville was where country music was celebrated. Taylor would soon become part of this world, signing her first deal with Sony/ATV soon after.

Her first album, *Taylor Swift* (known in the fandom as *Debut*), was released in 2006. Taylor's first release, 'Tim McGraw', was an instant success in country music spaces. Swift's penmanship and expressive vulnerability was front and centre even in these early days. Swift was sixteen at the time of the release of her self-titled debut – young, hungry and naive. While she aspired to find success within the country music scene that was full of her own idols, she did not ever appear daunted by retaining her own unique voice.

Swift cultivated the development of a core and passionate fanbase. The fanbase held its first roots in a country music listener, but gradually haloed out to wider circles of those on the periphery. This is often the pattern in the development of fandoms, that the buzz of a dedicated inner circle will trickle out and capture the interest of someone who sits on the precipice – who might kind of like country music, or find special memory in one hit single, and so find themselves ready to dip their toe a little deeper. With Taylor Swift, if you're dipping your toe, you're never coming back out of that water. There is simply too much to offer.

That said, there is huge power to be found in the acquisition of a small but dedicated fanbase. The unwavering support they offer can cultimate in their passion and excitement broadening out into the mainstream and capturing the attention of possible new fans. Continuing on a fast-moving trajectory, Swift quickly rose to the top of the country music game, being awarded a CMT Music Award for Breakthrough Artist in 2007, as well as a Country Music Award for New Female Vocalist of the Year.

Then came *Fearless*. Her second album, it has sold 100 million copies. Swift stuck close to her country roots with *Fearless*, but upped the ante with catchy lyrics, storybook-like songs, and radio-ready hooks and vibes. Songs like 'Fifteen' and 'You Belong With Me' identified Taylor as one of us – not the popular girl or the cheerleader, but the awkward outsider who struggled to find love, who was intimidated by the big world outside of high school. And she told us all about it, using her music almost as a diary.

What she told us, we understood – because we were living through it too.

That honestly and vulnerability has set the scene for her decade-long relationship with her earlier fans. That sense that we know her, that we have access to the inner workings of her mind but also her authentic feelings, creates a bond that grows with every direct or indirect interaction, with every lyric that helps a fan feel seen or better understood. It is a bond unique to the Swifties and the relationship they share with Taylor, and it is nothing short of a phenomenon.

Indeed, it was only upwards momentum that Taylor Swift experienced in her first years as a music artist, gaining a loyal, growing fanbase relatively quickly, though it would be a while before it ballooned to its massive heights of the 2020s. Her young, fresh voice inspired and won over thousands, and as a young girl in her late teens, fame found her.

But with fame comes opinions, eyes on you, and drama.

The drama that found Taylor Swift early on in her career would haunt her for many years to come, and frame her as one of the most talked-about celebrities of the decade.

Who you are is not what you did

Let's jump, then, to the MTV Video Music Awards in 2009. At nineteen years old, Taylor Swift was nominated for her first mainstream music awards – and then her rising stardom was challenged, her confidence shattered in one move, by Kanye West. It's impossible to write an overview of Taylor Swift's public life without talking about Kanye. At that time, Kanye was at the height of his fame, and Taylor was a fan. In an impulsive moment from Kanye West, a rivalry between two celebrities began – something that would follow them both in the years that followed.

Let's set the scene: Taylor Swift is wearing a beautiful Grecian, sparkling silver full-length dress, her perfectly curled hair set in a relaxed updo, and her already-signature red lip present. She is awarded Best Female Music Video, and the camera pans to her shocked, open-mouthed, delighted face. We see stars like Pink in the audience smiling proudly at the next generation of young female artists being rewarded by the industry. As Taylor takes to the stage and begins her speech, there's a camera cut and suddenly Kanye is on stage too, taking the microphone from Taylor's hands to proclaim Beyoncé the deserving winner of the award. Beyoncé, in the audience, looks shocked and clearly uncomfortable.

This is when the booing begins. Swift reflects in her Netflix documentary, *Miss Americana*, that she had felt these boos were for her – her first big trophy snatched from her eager grasp before she even had a chance to celebrate it, and her young insecurity contributing to a feeling that she is not deserving, that the audience doesn't like her. This moment is uncomfortable to watch, and, at the time of writing, something West has never apologised for. Yet it is clearly a defining moment for the future of Taylor's career, as well as her sense of self and how she fits into the industry. It is ironic that a young girl who wrote about not fitting in with the cool kids could be given this huge opportunity, a spotlight to celebrate herself, and have it crushed by someone she admired.

The media couldn't get enough of talking about it, and thus the drama found Taylor Swift for the first time (and certainly not the last). In that particular moment, Taylor Swift became a representation of the stereotypical media vision of young women – innocent, fragile and somehow inferior to their male peers. It certainly reinvigorated the dedication of her fans, and made her industry presence more strongly felt.

Taylor returned to the VMAs stage the following year to perform 'Innocent', an album track on *Speak Now* that refers directly to the MTV Awards moment. A powerful reflection on forgiveness, it takes on new meaning in the 2020s as Kanye West's mental health has deteriorated in the public eye over the course of the last few years.

With the release of *Speak Now* also came a new Taylor Swift – by this point writing songs about not only Kanye but also ex-boyfriends who happened to be such recognisable celebrities, including John Mayer and Taylor Lautner. She became known in the media not just because of the man that humiliated her, but for the men she would date – she was now the ex-girlfriend who would tell tales on her failed relationships. *Speak Now* was written solely by Swift after accusations from the press and music journalists that she wasn't capable of writing her own music. She did, to her useful determined effect – meaning she wrote about what she knew, only to meet further criticism, judgement and pigeonholing. Such is the burden carried by successful women that Taylor spent the first years of her rise to fame under constant scrutiny, minimised by the media despite her talent.

Seemingly undeterred, Swift kept her chin up and her head down, innovating and progressing her sound and ambition. She set her sights higher – beyond just being marked as a girl who writes songs about mean men, her next chess move was to take her sound from country to pop. She would do it flawlessly, while she was it. That is not to say she has truly shaken off her identity as 'girlfriend', though it has perhaps matured to 'lover'.

On *Speak Now* and *Fearless*, Swift is a hopeless romantic. Early on in her career she sets herself up as an outlier:

Taylor was, and never has been, your average cool girl.

The film critic Nathan Rabin coined the term 'manic pixie dream girl' to explain the stock female character type created as a muse, solely to teach a male lead or ensemble 'to embrace life and its infinite mysteries and adventures'. He further describes the archetype as 'an all-or-nothing-proposition'. It became a huge influence on how young men saw young women (and how those young women saw themselves) in the noughties and early tens. Swift was one of the first young women to step forward and break through this fast-growing ideology – she was not defined by the men who loved her, even if the media was determined to make that the case.

Within the love stories and fantasies were the self-reflections and the inner feelings of a young girl. Taylor defined her own emotional states and needs in her music with great self-awareness for someone in their late teens, and her own role in the relationship took centre stage. It wasn't just about men – it was about how they made her feel, how she faced love and heartbreak, as well as life growing up. *Speak Now* gave us even more than *Fearless* in that respect, with deep introspection and reflection on the things that impacted Swift in her early twenties.

Those albums defined *my* early twenties, both featuring love songs and self-love songs, written by a Swift who was living, sharing and defining her own experiences in the young adult phase of her life. One particular song, 'Fifteen', speaks more accurately to the teen experience than any song I have heard over my years as a music lover – perfectly encapsulating first love and heartbreak, but more so the deep bonds of friendship that young adults feel and how shared bonds can so often create shared feelings. 'Fifteen' speaks directly to the high-school stage – a song that sounds innocent but shows deep introspection about these formative encounters and how they can shape us for the rest of our life. It is Swift at her finest, speaking to and for an audience that has never had a voice before in music: the teenage girl.

One of Swift's most powerful skills, and one that she would retain even beyond these early albums, is her ability to summarise a strong, deeply held feeling or moment in just a handful of words or lines. 'Fifteen' is not the only song

of hers that achieves this, of course, but maybe it is one of the first, and provides a now-famous Taylor Swift gut punch when remembering her friend's first intimate experience. The loss of 'girlhood' is something that Taylor comes back to time and again, and once again is a life experience that changes so many but is rarely lingered on in songwriting.

Alongside songs such as 'Fifteen' there are also songs that are pure fantasy. Swift is known for referencing fantasy and dreams – even now, her songs promise midnight musings, imagined folklore and 'what ifs'. 'Love Story' was one of the first tracks that saw Taylor deviate from country star to pop princess. There is, deliberately, something Shakespearian in its treatment – Romeo and Juliet, sneaking around in gardens, and honourable proposals made against a backdrop of supposedly forbidden love.

So, how do these two notions of young womanhood fit together and create a vision that has made me (and many others) a fan of Taylor Swift for many years? The idea that it is possible to be broken-hearted and fearless, that we can pick ourselves up after a fall and still fantasise about our next beloved beau is truly representative of how many young people live life. Our minds were, and still are, full of contradiction, fantasy and feeling. To be a vengeful woman is a moment away from being a heartbroken woman; to be provocative can travel hand in hand with feeling objectified; to find joy in dancing around your bedroom can happen five minutes before you sit down with a philosophy book to expand your mind. People are complicated, but somehow

Taylor Swift makes it look easy to encapsulate the human experience in minutes.

So how did our teen confidante become what she is today – a global superstar? Thanks to the rise of the quickfire, shorthand culture that we now live in both on and offline, the fandom describes Swift in godlike, definitive terms – she is no longer Taylor Alison Swift. She has ascended to Mother.

The phrase Mother, which has been adopted by fandoms and admirers on social media platforms such as TikTok, finds its origins in queer and drag cultures, which has also moved into the public domain in recent years. The *New York Times* says,

> *'It derives from the Black and Latino L.G.B.T.Q. ballroom scene, a queer subculture in which members are organized into so-called houses often led by a "mother".*
>
> *The word's current use, however, veers campier and is mostly used as a term of endearment for famous women with avid devotees.'*

The term as used in drag communities showcases a sense of parental or sisterly nurturing from a peer, an honoured title of someone who helps and supports young queens through their journey and growth. While it is indeed used by fandoms to describe a number of famous women, it has been latched onto by Swifties in particular. Why?

Well, simply, Taylor Swift has raised her fans. She has taught us how to master the comeback, how to find our voices even under scrutiny. While Taylor's earlier years solidified her as one to watch in the media as a seductress of celebrity men or young starlet with potential, her next moves put her in the same lane as some of the biggest stars in the world. Along the

'Taylor Swift
has raised her fans.

She has taught us how
to master the comeback,
how to find **our voices**
even under scrutiny.'

way, we, the Swifties, came with her. We knew there was so much more to Taylor Alison Swift than meets the eye.

Her artistry, her vision and her ambition are what make her one of a kind –

and with the help of her fans, what drove her to become a superstar.

CHAPTER 4

THE 1

How Taylor Swift Built an Empire

In 2014, something wild happened: Taylor Swift cut her hair.

I know what you're thinking . . . how is that wild? Actually, if you're as into fandom as I am, you get it. But I remember it like it was yesterday: gone were the long, innocent country-star curls, and in their place was a beautiful flicky, fringy, choppy bob.

This bob inspired multitudes of young women in their twenties to cut their hair. Author Holly Bourne recounted to me that, in 2014, upon arriving at a party with her friends who hadn't seen each other for months, every single one of them had visited their hairdresser and requested a 'Taylor Swift'. The bob wasn't just a haircut – it was symbolic.

It was a power move: the shedding of the Taylor Swift of the past, and the introduction of Taylor Swift the pop star.

Before this, *Red*. We will come back to *Red*, my most beloved Taylor Swift album, but for now all you need to know is that two songs started to change the path of Swift's place in the music arena and the charts. 'We Are Never Ever Getting Back Together' was the lead single from *Red*, and with wild speculation that this song and mega-hit 'I Knew You Were Trouble' were about 1D's very own (and much-beloved) Harry Styles, the internet went crazy. Could Swift be taking on the most beloved member of the hottest boyband in the world with her lyrics? The answer, actually, was no, neither of those songs were about Harry, but the public lapped it up. The *Red* Era saw Swift dressing as a ringmaster, surrounded by trapeze artists, mimes and *Alice in Wonderland*-esque dancers – an indication that she was determined to take the reins of her own image, and so be it if the circus happens around her.

Taylor Swift was taking back control, and fame would follow on her terms.

Before we knew it, Taylor Swift was a bona-fide pop idol, and along with the famous hair chop came 'Shake It Off'. 'Shake It Off' is pop music in its purest form, an unforgettable and persistent earworm of a song that you can't help but tap your toes to. It proved that Swift's incredible ear for music sits not only in her prowess with lyrics but also for making addictive chart hits. She could, and would, turn her attention to world domination – but she would have fun doing so. 'Shake It Off' directly responded to the haters – sure, she goes on too many dates, but she always comes back swinging. She might be irritating and insipid, but why not let it go and dance along with her?

Superfans will always argue that this was the *real* Taylor, the one that nobody had a chance to see with all the media headlines about her ex-boyfriends and jabs about her musical talent. 1989 Taylor brought her sense of wit, a slight wildness and – most importantly – her strong sense of identity, to the front.

Then came 'Blank Space'. I'm not so inclined to do a track-by-track rundown of all of Taylor's massive hits, but if 'Shake It Off' poked fun at Swift's reputation with the public, 'Blank Space' ripped up the rule book, chucked scarlet paint on the headlines and threw what remained directly at the media. Taylor wasn't playing around, but yet she *was* – she was setting out her stall, poking out her tongue *and* sticking a middle finger up to those that had judged her all at once. 'Blank Space' said, 'Fine, if you call me boy crazy, I'll show you a bunny boiler. I'll make sure this song gets stuck in your head for the rest of time, and teach you who I really am at the same time.'

With the refrain of 'Boys only want love if it's torture, don't say I didn't warn ya', Swift solidified her move from twee country music singer to bold global pop star. Importantly, she kept every single young girl who travelled there with her onside – growing up at the same time as Taylor and heeding her important warning:

BOYS SUCKED,
and girls would, in the end, come out of heartache as victors.

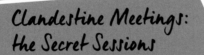

Clandestine Meetings: the Secret Sessions

With 1989 came the birth of the Secret Sessions. Also introduced in the 1989 Era, the Secret Sessions marked Taylor's most personal connection with fans yet.

What were they? And why do they matter?

The year 2014 marks a time period in which Taylor was not only changing her output dramatically, but also when she became visibly available online. Tumblr was a highly populated platform for Taylor Swift, posting updates, smart quips and reshares of fan content. She would comment on fan posts and take full advantage of the power of the 'like' button, sending fans into a delighted spin to be given the digital approval of their biggest idol.

It's kind of like TikTok today – but also TOTALLY DIFFERENT. There's always huge excitement when Taylor (or Taylor's account at least) likes or comments on a fan post today, but back in 2014 the access we had to our celebrities was so much more minimal, as 'X' and Instagram were mere babies, twinkles in the eye of their creators. Tumblr was a fan space. It wasn't for the celebs! To paraphrase *Mean Girls*, 'They don't even go here!' But Taylor did.

It was like she was collecting information from the inside track, delighting in fan theories and commentary. Taylor was right there, and you never knew when she would pop up. She was putting in the work, the time and the effort to get to know her fans, and give them what they wanted.

The first Secret Sessions were held in September and October 2014 across venues in the US and UK. Swift, aided by Taylor Nation, curated eighty-nine fans – of course – to attend each event. The fans didn't know exactly where they were going, but they knew something big was about to happen.

And where *were* they going? To one of Taylor's homes, to listen first to *1989*, with Taylor Swift herself. Video clips of the Secret Sessions show Taylor nervously hiding in the backyard of her mum's house, baking cookies in her own oven. It's unthinkable now that at her level of stardom Taylor could simply walk into a room in her own home, filled with fans, and shout 'HI GUYYYYYSSSSS!' from around a corner before sitting down and playing a whole album – without invoking any spoilers, song leaks, or worse: where she lives, her address or access to her most private spaces.

In the Secret Sessions videos and photos, Taylor can be seen dancing around with her fans, hugging and chatting, letting them hold and interact with her beloved cats. The Secret Sessions created an incredible opportunity – fan service like no other, word of mouth excitement and hype, and album promotion marketing around the drop itself. These fans proclaimed 1989 the best thing they'd ever heard – and Taylor herself the nicest person, their friend, their confidante. She kept our secrets safe, while rewarding us with some of hers, and we would keep them until we could scream about it from the rooftops.

The Secret Sessions were developed by Taylor her and her team in the time of 'word of mouth' marketing, a powerful form of buzz building and self-promotion. They happened in the *Fifty Shades of Grey* era, when the most desired asset was the approval of the everyday consumer. Pre-TikTok, pre-Spotify being a part of everyday life, this kind of awareness was hard to come by, and ever harder for brands to manifest. The Secret Sessions were genius, showing early on that not only was Taylor truly dedicated to rewarding her fanbase, she was a smart, shrewd businesswoman.

Another gift to the fandom was Swiftmas. Taylor ended 2014 by personally sourcing and wrapping gifts for her biggest fans, delivering them in time for Christmas. The result is on YouTube – a video with over 20 million views: Swift is shown in a relaxed sweatshirt and Santa hat curating these parcels, complete with handwritten cards and thoughtful messages. This footage is followed by videos of the fan recipients crying, screaming, unable to believe that their idol cared this much about *them*. Of course, it's a nice moment – but it's also there for us all to watch, to evidence that Taylor Swift is the nicest celebrity in the world, ever, in case you hadn't realised before.

The Secret Sessions and Swiftmas showcase Taylor's unstoppable work ethic. If she's not performing a three-hour show, or releasing back-to-back pandemic albums and re-records, she's online, seeing us – seeing *you* – and finding ways to make that message spread more widely to ensure that more people see *her*, rewarding her most loyal fans.

I Can See You: Easter eggs

Speaking of fan loyalty and messages: we have to talk about Easter eggs.

Easter eggs as a cultural notion have existed since the late 1970s, when software development director of Atari, Steve Wright, referenced the fun of finding little secret messages and clues in video games as being 'like an Easter egg hunt'.

Taylor has been gifting us secret messages and clues for as long as I can remember. It has intensified with the rise of social media, but Taylor has clearly always enjoyed creating a sense of fan interaction beyond live performances and secret meetings. Telling us how she feels in songs is not enough – she wants us to interact with her, to pick up the breadcrumbs she drops and to feel them between our fingers. If Taylor can't reach us all in person, she can – and does – speak to us through other mediums.

These mediums are plentiful: capitalised letters spelling out bonus phrases in album liner notes and lyrics; coloured nails or particular hairstyles in her street style teasing at her next Era; or music-video imagery hinting at release dates and complicated numerology, of which Swift is a self-confessed enthusiast. These Easter eggs have intensified in later years, with the huge joy this brings the fandom made clear, and they have become a staple part of how Taylor connects with us and intensifies the parasocial relationship we share.

#TaylorSwiftIsOverParty

Perhaps the most notorious time period follows next. After great efforts to bring the real Taylor to the forefront of her artistry, at the new height of her fame there was a massive fallout. The villain? That's right, the return of Kanye West, with a more cunning scheme than the last.

Upon the release of Kanye's track, 'Famous', the public went berserk over a line that referenced Taylor and stated that he made 'that bitch' famous. Taylor clapped back immediately at this insulting, misogynistic dig, and so West (and then-wife Kim Kardashian) released a secretly recorded conversation with Swift, in which she seems to be excited and enthusiastic, giving her blessing for the song to be released.

The masses piled on instantly. Of course Taylor Swift was a fake, a duplicitous witch who was not to be trusted! We knew it all along!! Thanks to Kim Kardashian's now famous tweets in support of her husband, Taylor was branded a snake. #TaylorSwiftIsOverParty trended worldwide for days on end, her social media overrun with serpent emojis and scathing comments. The higher you rise, the harder you fall.

What followed was Taylor's disappearance from social media and the public eye for almost a full year. When she returned, it was Swift's *reputation* Era that came with her, accompanied by proof that West's video was falsified and out of context. *reputation* saw Taylor give her first enthusiastic 'fuck you' to the industry, the media and the intense public expectations placed on her. She hit the refresh button on what it meant to be Taylor Swift.

She tells us in 'Look What You Made Me Do', the first single from *reputation*, that indeed she has changed: the old Taylor is dead, replaced with a new, angry version of our favourite pop star. While this fall from grace was undoubtedly gutting and character testing for Swift, it seemed to strip another layer of polite people-pleasing from her character. Out of a year away from the public eye, with a new media-shy boyfriend and a determination to come back with a bang, emerged a more mature, headstrong woman.

Taylor Swift became a rebel, and reputation redefined her career again – propelling her to do the thing she knew best:

trust her instincts, back herself and stand up and fight.

Following the #TaylorSwiftIsOverParty, we saw a new Taylor who put her fame second, her desire for universal acceptance tinged with an understanding that friendship and loyalty were more important than parties and popularity. It was at that time that we saw the girl gang formed around the 1989 Era dissolve, replaced by the chosen few friends who have always stood by her: namely, Blakey Lively, the Haim sisters, Gigi Hadid and Selena Gomez.

Selena and Taylor's friendship has stayed the test of time. Both growing into the music industry at the same age around the same time, and experiencing exposing public break-ups and takedowns, Selena represents everything we want for Taylor: understanding, warmth and unconditional love. The knowledge that Taylor has a friend like that, and to see the two champion each other through the highs, and console through the lows, helps us to see Taylor as human: a star, but also a sidekick and hype girl. We will always keep our own girlies close, reminded by Taylor and Selena that you need your bestie more than you need your boyfriends. Similarly, Taylor's ability to build on and retain professional respect and friendships with artists such as Beyoncé, demonstrates how highly Taylor values her relationships. In particular with Beyoncé, both women often strive to mutually demonstrate their admiration and fondness for the other – sometimes even to make a clear point to their individual fanbases about ignoring media rumours and alleged rivalries.

Taylor Swift has grown up before our eyes – and we have grown with her.

It is this Taylor Swift that has gained a huge fanbase of inspired young people. Her own fight has led to an army of defence – Swifties who will loyally follow her every move. Taylor can now travel from country to pop to indie, to whatever style of music she sees fit. Her extensive back catalogue is to be celebrated and applauded, for it is this musical shapeshifting that has seen her lauded as one of the greatest artists of all time. Where she goes, we will follow.

Dave Faubert
(Founder of Swiftogeddon)

What is Swiftogeddon?

It is quite simply a club night of nothing but Taylor Swift songs. One after the other, back to back, no repeats, no other artists. We have shows all across the UK, for people to come and celebrate Taylor Swift.

When and why did you set it up?

When I first started it up, a lot of venues just couldn't get their heads round it. But I had this crazy idea, and the Moth Club in London took a chance on it. I thought if I can get a hundred people there, it'll be great. We then ended up doing another one in Manchester during Pride weekend, and it started expanding. Now we're nationwide, putting on twenty shows a month. We have people who've never been to club nights – but they come for Taylor's music.

When I started it, everyone thought it was a stupid idea, including myself. In my eyes, all I'm doing is adding value to Taylor's fanbase and her music. We're firing up the fans and, hopefully, getting a few new ones on board – people who might come along with their mates and discover her. We're very careful about putting on a great night: the messaging, the music we choose, it's all thought about every time and the setlist is different every time. My job is to make a great safe space to celebrate Taylor's music, which fundamentally is what it all boils down to. That's the rock a great fandom is built on. If the tunes weren't great, nobody would give a monkey's.

Why do fans go to Swiftageddon?

There's a few reasons: obviously they love Taylor Swift. I think they also love the night itself because it's a lovely group of people. It's a very safe and joyous atmosphere. It's a safe space to just let yourself go: there's no judgement, and we work hard to make everyone comfortable from the minute they're there. Sing along, jump around, enjoy yourself. Don't worry about what anyone else thinks: that's what it's all about.

Are you a Taylor Swift fan – and why?

Yes, I am. She's a genius songwriter, that's the main reason I like her. I admire her as a businesswoman – the re-recordings are an amazing example of that. How do you capture lightning in a bottle twice? But she's done it. She's an artist at the absolute peak of her powers. She makes great decisions, and she works incredibly hard. I don't think she's ever got a major decision wrong.

When you think of Taylor Swift fans, what do you think of?

They're just lovely – and they care so much about her and her music. The ones I meet are all very genuine. Taylor makes music for outsiders, and the Swifties generally might not be the most confident, popular people – but they love her music and they love sharing it with other people. People might come to Swiftogeddon on their own and they'll make friends. They're a very welcoming bunch.

CHAPTER 5

FEARLESS (TAYLOR'S VERSION)

How Reclaiming Her Masters Empowered a Fanbase?

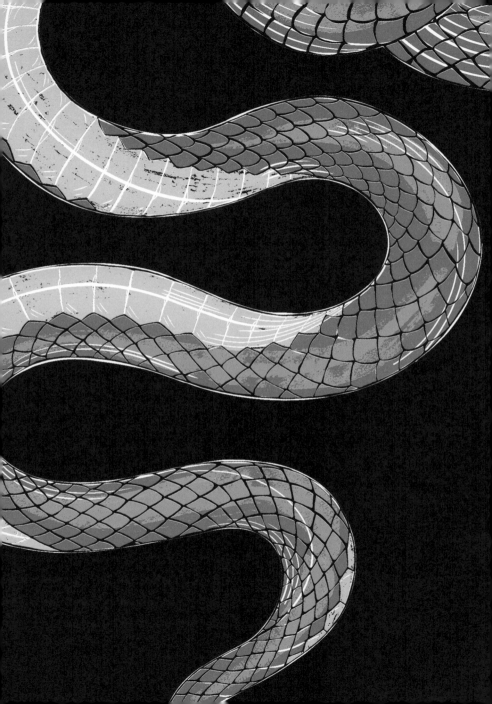

The *reputation* Era brought us a new Taylor Swift – one who was powerful, unstoppable and with a strong sense of moral retribution. In 2019 this power was put to the test publicly, thanks to a new villain: Scooter Braun.

Music masters are, simply, an artist's original final mixes. They are usually retained by the record label, who consult with the artist for the right to license those recordings to be used on soundtracks, in advertisements and live recordings, and ultimately give the owner full control over the use of the music. It is typical that these would be owned by a label and it feels typical that Taylor Swift, as a teenager signing her first contract, would not question the handing over of her rights to the experts.

As Taylor Swift grew in strength as an artist, so did her vocalness within the industry – she started to stand up for what she felt was right, for artists to receive credit where it was due. In 2014, Taylor went against the status quo to remove her music from streaming platform Spotify. In the *New York Journal*, she declared, 'It's my opinion that music should not be free and my prediction is that individual artists and their labels will someday decide what an album's price point is.' This was the first time she publicly took a stand against a big industry player and she removed her music from Spotify for four years, only returning it as a 'reward' to fans when her album sales hit 100 million copies.

In 2015, during the release cycle of 1989, Taylor Swift wrote an open letter to Apple. This letter is particularly interesting and gives us an insight into Taylor's character and principles when it comes to her artistry. It is not the only letter we will see from her with this intent. Newly launched streaming service, Apple Music, had a clause in which artists would not receive royalties during new members' free three-month trials. Taylor objected strongly to this, and took to her social media for the first time to demand a response to her concerns, with a letter entitled

'To Apple, Love Taylor':

I'm sure you are aware that Apple Music will be offering a free 3-month trial [. . .] I'm not sure you know that Apple Music will not be paying writers, producers, or artists for those three months. I find it to be shocking, disappointing, and completely unlike this historically progressive and generous company.

This is not about me. [. . .] This is about the new artist or band that has just released their first single and will not be paid for its success.

This strongly worded statement made it clear that Taylor was not doing this for her own endeavours – it placed her as a white knight, pledging to support her still-developing colleagues in the music industry. It also sets out her stall as an artist not afraid to get personal when talking about unfair business strategy:

> These are not the complaints of a spoiled, petulant child. These are the echoed sentiments of every artist, writer and producer in my social circles who are afraid to speak up publicly because we admire and respect Apple so much. We simply do not respect this particular call.

It's fascinating to see the repositioning of Taylor in this letter – no longer is she an innocent and sweet country star who will have her dues stolen from her grasp. No, she is a businesswoman who is making it clear that she is well aware of her public perception as young and naive; and she will speak up when something is not okay by her:

> I say to Apple with all due respect, it's not too late to change this policy and change the minds of those in the music industry who will be deeply and gravely affected by this. We don't ask you for free iPhones. Please don't ask us to provide you with our music for no compensation.

Suffice to say that her rise above the parapet worked. Apple changed their policy, and Taylor and her team struck up an ongoing relationship with them across marketing and advertising. We, the fans, gained much from this experience, introduced to a

Taylor Swift that didn't only speak up for us and our feelings, she spoke up for what is right.

In 2018, it was announced that after thirteen years (of course), Taylor was to change labels from Big Machine to Republic Records, and that from *Lover* onwards all her album masters would be owned by her as part of this deal. Little was said about Big Machine apart from expressed gratitude, but before long it became clear that there was conflict. In 2019, Big Machine sold her music as part of a business deal, and so began the start of a much larger battle. Enter: Scooter Braun.

For Taylor Swift to be able to have any input on how her previous six albums were put out to third parties, or even performed live, or sampled, she would have to defer to Scooter Braun and Big Machine. She openly stated that she did not want her music – and how it was used – in the hands of Scooter: a man she told us had bullied, controlled and belittled her Despite several attempts to purchase her masters, Taylor had been refused.

Scooter Braun and Big Machine have issued statements that differ from Swift's perspective, stating that Taylor was offered many opportunities to discuss the ownership issue - with Braun ultimately defining the rift as a 'misunderstanding' in a now-deleted Instagram post.

So, what next? Well, if Taylor wasn't allowed to buy her own music, she would re-record it, and make it hers again.

To be an A-lister does not come easily, and we can never truly know what happens behind record-label doors. We can likely assume that there is a constant struggle between wanting to hold authority over your public image while pleasing your label. Concerns like this aren't unique to being famous – we've all wanted to challenge the status quo at work or school at some point.

But in the world of fame, where the stakes are high and your career success attached to so many people, how do you rise above? It's not new for musicians to push the agenda, be rebellious or fight for their rights, but with Taylor, one of the most prominent artists of our generation, she has without question surprised people with her defiance in business, her determination to achieve what she feels is right.

Weaponising her fanbase

The reclamation of Taylor's masters has played a key role in the development of her fanbase. The *(Taylor's Version)* version of Taylor comes as a direct result of a naive past, growing up as a musician and learning on the job very much in the public eye. With this move, she clearly tells her fans

to find power in ourselves, to trust our gut and set our own standard if we need to.

Indeed, her fanbase was involved in the decision to re-record her masters from the beginning. Most of Taylor's announcements are now led by her social media platforms, meaning that we the fans hear from her first about what she is up to. This is true of the re-records, and Taylor's excitement over them meant we were excited for them. It was also something that no artist had been seen to do before (certainly not in this generation), and further evidence that Taylor was innovative, brave and as passionate about her music as we were.

Along the way, though, there were further hurdles to

jump, and Taylor was to let us know about that, too. In 2019, prior to the American Music Awards, she took to Tumblr with another letter, this time to her fans, entitled, 'Don't know what else to do':

Scott Borchetta told my team that they'll allow me to use my music only if I do these things: If I agree to not re-record copycat versions of my songs next year (which is something I'm both legally allowed to do and looking forward to) and also [. . .] that I need to stop talking about him and Scooter Braun.
I feel very strongly that sharing what is happening to me could change the awareness level for other artists . . .The message being sent to me is very clear. Basically, be a good little girl and shut up. Or you'll be punished.

This is WRONG. Neither of these men had a hand in the writing of those songs. They did nothing to create the relationship I have with my fans. So this is where I'm asking for your help.
Please let Scott Borchetta and Scooter Braun know how you feel about this. Scooter also manages several artists who I really believe care about other artists and their work. Please ask them for help with this – I'm hoping that maybe they can talk some

sense into the men who are exercising tyrannical control over someone who just wants to play the music she wrote.

[...]

I just want to be able to perform MY OWN music. That's it. I've tried to work this out privately through my team but have not been able to resolve anything.

[...]

I love you guys and I thought you should know what's been going on.

This letter created ripples across the internet, with people questioning whether Taylor's relationship with her fans was as parasocial as theirs with her. Taylor at this stage had a huge, dedicated fanbase that would go into bat for her. Choosing to ask them to help her cause could be powerful, but could it be risky too? In a *Billboard* interview with Scooter Braun published in 2022, the music mogul spoke about 'weaponising fans'.

He said: 'The artists I work with have very large fanbases. You don't do that ... There's people in that fanbase who have mental health issues. There's families involved, and I think that's very dangerous.'

Scooter Braun and Scott Borchetta have stated they have

received death threats as a result of the battle over Taylor Swift's masters. Ultimately, with a huge fanbase comes great responsibility. On the other side of that, the reason Taylor Swift fans love her so much is for her openness, her transparency and feeling that we understand her. This extension of her music into her business acumen, her moral stance, only makes us feel closer to her. The power of this creates even more support, and enables her to do such things as re-record her albums. We will support her, no matter what she chooses to do.

The devil works hard . . . but Taylor works harder

The first release of Taylor's masters coincided with the COVID-19 lockdown. During the lockdown, Taylor put out two albums: *folklore* and *evermore*, two masterpieces that gave her the musical credibility she – and much of the fanbase – so strongly desired. Both albums were praised highly by music journalists, Taylor Swift cynics and, of course, her loyal fans. They presented us with introspective music that perfectly set the tone for the prisons we were all in during the pandemic.

Taylor once again was with us, even when nobody else was.

It is this credibility that added further weight to the re-releases, and Taylor's future domination of the music world. The final missing piece of the puzzle: Taylor had proved to the wider world that she could write not one, but two albums that put artistry first – albums that wouldn't need the noise and drama of a world tour, because the world was out of reach; albums that focused solely on creativity, reflection and music. These albums are unquestionably brilliant, and so the naysayers finally sat back, relaxed and wept appreciatively along with the superfans.

Just when we all thought Taylor could not be more unstoppable, *Fearless (Taylor's Version)* came on 21 April 2021. The release of *Fearless* was a litmus test. How would a re-release be received? Would there be hype? Could there be as much excitement as with a brand-new album? Well, *Fearless* saw a quieter response than the re-records to follow – but it played an important role in setting up fan rituals that have stuck, including a forensic assessment of pre-release clues and Easter eggs, live responses to the new versions of the tracks recorded and posted on social media, and honouring each release with themed outfits, videos and vibes.

If you're a fan who's been around since the original

releases, it was an opportunity to be a historical guide – educating newer Swifties on the characters and significant features on the album, while they formed their own opinions and made their own emotional connections to songs that changed my life a decade ago.

Then there are the 'vault' tracks. Swift had often seeded the notion that unheard songs were on the cutting-room floor. Now she had the chance to offer us her version, those songs would be returned to the album in the form of vault tracks. The vault tracks give fans new songs to pore over, like a mini-album within an album. They also give journalists something new to review, and the opportunity to make new videos – complete with Easter eggs to drive fans wild with excitement.

Fearless might have been the litmus test, but it sold over half a million copies in 2021.

However it was the re-release of *Red (Taylor's Version)* in November that year that sent the world spinning out of orbit into a Taylor Swift-coded, scarlet-shaded frenzy.

Red, in its first iteration, is the first Taylor Swift album release I remember. It is the album that turned me into a diehard Swiftie. I remember the first time I listened to it, on my crappy laptop in a rented flat in South London. It coincided with the most significant period of growth in my mid-twenties. There were a lot of highs, and a lot of lows

– dating sucked, I was broke, work was intensely hard. The emotional challenges of adulting were harder than I could have imagined.

But I had *Red*. Heartening, toe-tapping, sobfest-inducing *Red*.

Back then we didn't have TikTok. We didn't have 'X'. We didn't have DeuxMoi. There was a lot of mystery, and far fewer people to play detective with. Any examination, reflection or suspicion we had about Taylor's life at that time was kept private, just between me . . . and Taylor.

Red marked the beginning of Taylor's breakout into the mainstream. It is more or less a perfect album. She wouldn't be my heartfelt secret much longer. 'We Are Never Ever Getting Back Together', '22' and 'I Knew You Were Trouble' were big hits. Still I sat, while I could, and experienced *Red* with quiet and private intimacy, savouring every moment and every word.

F**k the Patriarchy

I remember it All Too Well

The first time I heard 'All Too Well' felt like the first time I had heard music. In 'All Too Well', Taylor told me about her heartbreak in real time, in poetry, in words that were familiar to me, with feelings that I had felt time and time again by this point in my young life. Taylor was twenty-three years old when *Red* was released; I was twenty-six, and we were both rooted firmly in our feelings. Taylor knew how to articulate my heartbreaks and disappointments better than I did. 'All Too Well' is a special song, because it tells in great detail of an experience that Taylor had, but it feels like it belongs to you, the listener. We also know, through implication and visual hints, that the song is almost certainly about A-list actor Jake Gyllenhaal (though he denies that it has anything to do with him in a recent interview with *Esquire*) – the ability to visualise the intended heartbreaker of this song added weight and meaning, and it also added some drama.

Was this what it was like to date a celebrity? How dare Jake Gyllenhaal take Taylor's scarf and never give it back? What an asshole. Those were thoughts I had as I listened, while also relating it to my own assholes who took my stuff and never called me again.

Returning back to 2021 – *Red (Taylor's Version)* was an anticipated moment in Swift's schedule that year – and there were many coveting fans who couldn't wait for the wider world to experience *Red*. I had many friends, newer Swifties, who had never heard the entirety of it, and I promised them greatness.

What I had not promised them, but what Taylor gave us, is a *ten-minute version* of 'All Too Well'. Long had a Swiftie urban legend circulated that a longer version of the song existed. To have not only confirmation but a promise that we would get to hear it, was the Holy Grail of the fandom.

The anticipation of the fanbase – equal parts excited and nervous to hear such a long piece of music – flooded out into the mainstream. The bold audacity to promise a ten-minute version of a ten-year-old song hit the wider public with intrigue. The media soon picked up on the hype, and threw Jake Gyllenhaal back into the room (you might say under the bus) with us too. 'All Too Well (10 Minute Version)' soon became one of the most anticipated songs of the year, despite it being a decade old.

Let's get technical for a moment. To take a five-minute song from your cult catalogue and craft it into something twice as long, actually dissecting the song throughout and adding in new verses, refrains, bridges and brand-new musical constructions, is nothing short of genius. Paired with brutal, gut-punching lyrics, Taylor has never been braver in her musical efforts. We hear for the first time not only of autumnal drives and painful break-ups – we hear more clearly about emotional trauma: broken sacred oaths, about shame and secrecy, about the starved body of a heartbroken young girl.

These are not the things that we ask society to pay attention to or care about – the deep ruin that can be inflicted on young people in early relationships is so often ignored, minimised and even fetishised by the wider media today.

Taylor once again becomes our voice, unafraid to tell us how it really is, how it really feels.

Taylor Swift's new version of 'All Too Well' also goes to great lengths to make clear the disturbing age difference between Swift and Gyllenhaal when they dated, and how deeply this impacted her, how inappropriate it was. The release of the longer song was accompanied by a music video – *All Too Well: The Short Film* – that clearly depicts the imbalance of the relationship, played out by Sadie Sink and Dylan O'Brien who present the same gap in age.

To return to the weaponisation of a fanbase, this time Taylor Swift didn't have to write us a letter to ask for retribution to be actioned. Instead, she wrote us a song, and let the autumn leaves fall as they may. Jake Gyllenhaal's name was everywhere, his social media comments overrun

by the red scarf emoji. Taylor had won something back from that relationship, after years, with an army of loyal soldiers who would fight to help plaster her wounds, protect her trauma – in hope of somehow healing our own. Jake Gyllenhaal was no longer just that guy from *Donnie Darko*: he was all of our exes.

None of this is for me to place a moral position on. Unlike Scooter, Jake stayed silent apart from denying he is the basis of the song. We can't know how he felt when this was all happening – perhaps it didn't impact him in any way.

This is the most Taylor has ever indulged in her own hype. Imagine if you could galvanise millions of dedicated fans to mutually mourn with; to get the upper hand through an army of willing fighters. Heartbreaks change us, and solace and sympathy fuel us. Taylor Swift has access to this on an unimaginable scale.

Red (TV) marked the beginning of an upswell of activity on TikTok. 'All Too Well (10 Minute Version)' saw scores of live reacts. Superfans have often filmed themselves hearing a new single for the first time – 'Look What You Made Me Do', a song that signified a huge change in Taylor's character, saw an influx of reaction videos. The 'mic drop' moment in which Taylor emphatically declares the old her *dead*, saw fans gasping with glee, jaws dropped – we were gagged.

ATW was this but on a new scale. Fans filmed themselves sat eagerly in front of their smartphones while they took it all in – smiling nervously at first, sobbing uncontrollably by the end. These unrehearsed, undirected reactions instantly went viral – they were unfiltered expressions of fandom and human emotion, demonstrating just how much Taylor made us feel, and how much she made us feel seen. Her trauma reflected our own, and the world got to see how strongly Taylor's music could make us feel, and how healing it could be.

Taylor Swift is excellent at creating these 'mic drop' moments in her songwriting. It lends itself beautifully to social media, which gives an outlet to fans to express and share their excitement and passion. The response to 'All Too Well', the ability to bear witness to fans experiencing music in real time, is unique to the time we live in now, the way we are experiencing and consuming content. It is becoming a trademark part of Swift's album releases.

Why does it make us feel so moved, so seen and understood, to see other fans filming themselves listening to songs? It is a testament to how fan communities reach each other, and validate each other. Taylor's music is personal and revealing – through her songwriting she touches our hearts and souls, and to see that play out beyond one's own mind is beautiful. To see real people experience their own feels and personal responses that may differ from yours is educating, and empathy creating. Music, and how our peers feel about it, helps us learn about each other. The ATW videos on TikTok

'Her trauma reflected our own, and the world got to see how strongly Taylor's music could make us feel, and how healing it could be.'

are part of this. Fans filming on their own, or seeking solace in group settings, are putting their hearts on their sleeves, just like Taylor does.

But we feel heartbreak for Taylor, too. There are viral TikTok videos of young girls sobbing and shaking as they hear the song unravel; hearing of Swift starving herself out of grief, being embarrassed and dismissed, being denied the love that we all feel she deserves. Ultimately, the fans just want Taylor to find happiness. We have been on her hunt for it with her.

Swift's songwriting has, over the years, become more honest and raw. Her fanbase and her success have validated her musical direction, helping her gaining confidence in her vision and her talent, but is it also because she sees that this is what her fans want and respond to? Is there a benefit to Swift's heartbreak going viral?

The release of *Taylor's Versions* have allowed for experimentation, to try to understand how on a new, almost instant, and ever-growing scale, Taylor can reach her fans and share her music and her life with them. *Red (TV)*'s viral nature created a buzz around the re-releases that has become part of how the fandom now operates. Easter eggs for which re-recording is next are littered in every new release, in the street style Swift adopts – a blue nail polish could equal 1989 (TV), a snakeskin dress hints at *reputation (TV)*. Why does it matter?

What we do know is that a large proportion of Taylor's fans are young women, teens coming into their first days of adulthood, feeling seen by the lyrics put in front of them and the honesty of experiences they share.

Those young fans are so important not only to Taylor personally, but to her success.

So why are they so often dismissed by society, and why is the content they love given less value by the wider world?

CHAPTER 6

ONLY THE YOUNG

Why Don't We Care About Teenagers?

We have all experienced teendom.

Some of you reading this might be in the thick of your young adulthood. It can be one of the most exhilarating, explorative and exhausting times of one's life. Full of new experiences, new feelings, experimentation, rebellion, rage, romance – being a teenager is truly a time to remember. But why does it seem that so many adults have forgotten about it, and dismiss it as a time best forgotten?

Taylor Swift became famous at just sixteen years old. As we have said, many of her songs then (and now) express and share the concerns of young girls, because that was what she was experiencing at the time. That seems obvious. It also feels pretty obvious that while she found an audience of country music fans fairly instantly, she started quite low down the ranking of what might be considered 'serious' music. But around the time of her rise to fame, what else were people listening to? What was topping the charts, and why was it given more standing in society?

Music was split fairly evenly – there was dance-heavy R&B paired with sexy, upbeat pop music such as Beyoncé, Rihanna, Black Eyed Peas, Girls Aloud, the Pussycat Dolls and Christina Aguilera. Then there was an upsurge of male-led indie music from the likes of Arctic Monkeys, The Kooks, Snow Patrol and The Killers. Reality TV music contestants were creating new slots in the industry – the likes of Leona Lewis, Will Young, and more comedic acts such Chico and Jedward were all entering the music charts, put there by teen and family audiences.

We know that One Direction won the hearts of thousands if not millions of teens during their twelve weeks of live performances on *The X Factor*, and we also know that all five of the boys – Harry, Liam, Louis, Niall and Zayn – continue to showcase enormous gratitude to their fanbase. We have seen in recent years young people take their fandom and create megastars, famous beyond their wildest dreams. BTS, a K-pop band made up of the uber talented Jin, Suga, J-Hope, RM, Jimin, V, and Jungkook, are a modern day 1D, albeit from a different part of the world. Their fanbase, the BTS 'Army', undoubtedly helped put them where they are. Comments can often be seen on BTS' fantastic music videos on YouTube, fans rallying one another to raise the view by another million by way of sheer will power and servitude. It is BTS' Army that brought the band success outside of Korea, making them one of the most famous boybands in the world today. This passion can also be seen in the fanbases of other teen-idolised bands and artists such as Blackpink, Conan Grey and 5SOS. Chart success is no longer just decided by those sitting behind big desks – whether those desks are shown primetime on ITV or not.

So why do we so often dismiss teenagers, and the music and media they respond to, when they possess the power to create stars?

Sick-lit

In 2013 the *Daily Mail* wrote an article headlined:

> *'The "sick-lit" books aimed at children: It's a disturbing phenomenon. Tales of teenage cancer, self-harm and suicide . . .'*

We all know that the *Daily Mail* in particular has a penchant for taking an intentionally divisive view of anything and everything. We live in a world where clicks are key, where dividing society with moral questions is how the media remains relevant.

Unfortunately, the notion of sick-lit offers us a strong example – beyond the shiny, glittery world of music and performers – of how the lives and concerns of teenagers are all too often not taken seriously in the media's reception of their art. Somehow, we have created a world in which a whole generation of people are simply not allowed to have art that accurately reflects their feelings – whether that be happiness, or in the case of these books, hardship. Before the days of TikTok and social media coverage, those appraising these stories, songs and idols were not often the target audience.

There are a number of groundbreaking young adult (YA) novels cited in the *Daily Mail* article – including *The Fault in Our Stars* by John Green, which has sold more than 23 million copies worldwide. Also included is Jay Asher's *13 Reasons Why*, now a viral Netflix series with a huge teen fanbase. *13 Reasons* is not without its issues, and has been challenged frequently for its appropriateness in general. *The Fault in Our Stars* too became a huge movie, as YA (young adult) fiction adaptations often are. *The Hunger Games*, *Twilight*, *The Summer I Turned Pretty* and more all originated as books for teens.

The *Daily Mail* article, while creating a buzz of conversation about how we safeguard young people from the content they consume, failed to actually put any young people at the centre of the conversation, to ask how they felt about all this. This is often the case. We spend a lot of time talking about the needs of teens, and not a lot of time including them in the conversation.

The fact is this: teenage lives are not that different from those of adults. I will always fight for teens to have access to content that reflects their real experience, without patronising it. The same is true for the power of Taylor Swift. People use music, books, movies and social media to help us make sense of the things we learn in life. Teenagers live through heartbreak, it is normal that they may experience depression, mental health challenges and self-harm and, yes, some may have sex, whether that is consenting or not. They experience health problems and identity challenges, and they work through many new existential feelings from the meaning of life to a fear of death.

While it is important to have these stories told, it is important that they are told properly and responsibly. The extreme end of the spectrum of content for teens lies within the likes of 'sick-lit' – and the television shows and movies inspired by the genre – and we should know that those stories have been sensitivity checked or told with consultancy from expert organisations and young people, too.

Vampire

In a world where women are so often pitted against each other, the comparisons of Taylor Swift and her female musician peers are endless.

Olivia Rodrigo has received similar acclaim for her musical style, first releasing her truthful, witty and smart music at just seventeen years old. A Disney kid, Olivia Rodrigo is very much a 'fanmade' celebrity, going viral on TikTok and Instagram before releasing the hugely

anticipated hit 'drivers license'. Taylor Swift has been cited as a big inspiration of Olivia's, and at first this association was seen to be positive and exciting. Taylor and Olivia have been photographed together, and Olivia credited Taylor formally as inspiration for the song 'déjà vu'. This credit has fuelled the rumour mill, sparking discussion that there has been tension. Those 'in the know' state that Rodrigo has been humiliated by Swift, even positing that multiple songs on Rodrigo's second album are about Taylor, including 'vampire', which speaks passionately of duplicity and betrayal.

Famous women, particularly young women, often fall victim to accusations of girlfights, pettiness and rivalries. This is almost always a creation of the media, without any input from the involved parties – a condition that haunts young people who are in the public eye.

Taylor Swift's music in early days was consistently reduced to a less mature or less serious venture. If there is such a thing as 'music for young people' and if Taylor Swift is – or at least, was – defined as overemotional, a vengeful ex and simply only concerned with the needs of young girls then . . . why is that a problem? How can it be possible that so many of us experience all of the feelings that Swift so clearly expresses, and that that doesn't matter to society?

Before she transcended to the power she has today, many female-coded pejoratives were thrown around when it came to Taylor's first outings. 'Ex girlfriend' has so commonly been used as a jibe or a jab at her credibility. But . . . haven't we all been heartbroken? Haven't we all had to deal with being an ex-something to someone?

'Petty' is another one. Loaded with implication, 'petty' and 'vengeful' are so often thrown in the ring when talking about Taylor's music. Classic back catalogue songs such as 'Mean' and 'Better Than Revenge' are now finding new life with Swift's album rereleases – but it only takes a simple Google to find click-baiting articles about Taylor's 'top five' petty moments or high-school colleagues of Swift's claiming her as bitter and unlikeable.

So, again I ask – haven't we *all* felt vengeful? Haven't we all made petty comments, or privately thought up unfair assassinations of the people who wrong us? The fact that Taylor writes songs about this, and that young people respond to them with such heart, soul and devotion, tells us there's a place for them in our world. The fact that the world at that time rejected them shows us how misogyny in society continues to disrespect and discredit the experience of young women.

Let's look at 'Better Than Revenge' – a song not a million miles away from the lauded 'Misery Business' by Swift's peers and friends, the band Paramore. 'Better Than Revenge' is one of Taylor's most petty, vengeful songs. She was nineteen when she wrote it, so . . . that tracks. It tells of an ex-boyfriend and his icky new girlfriend, a total takedown by Taylor who declares this girl *'not a saint . . . not what you think, she's an actress'* and the now famous line, *'she's better known for the things that she does on the mattress'*. The 2023 re-record of this song offered Swift the opportunity to change that controversial lyric, and indeed she did. I like to think of BTR Taylor in a tongue-in-cheek sense as 'pre-feminism Taylor' – a younger woman more concerned and consumed by her own feelings than being responsible and adhering to girl code. She was learning – at the same time as her young audience.

I appreciate why it matters that artists like Taylor Swift use public platforms responsibly, but I also think that something can get lost in the process. Have we not all thought these thoughts? Is it not part of young adulthood to be mad and jealous and a bit of a brat? Does it matter if we put that brattiness into the public space to be observed by others?

It leads us to explore why we need our celebrities to be mindful of their words and their choices – Taylor Swift as a young, less famous woman in the mid-2000s could tell us to tell her ex-boyfriend's new girlfriend to suck it (which we all did with great glee, thinking of our own counterparts who ran off with our yucky exes). Taylor has always held adolescence close to her heart, clearly a pivotal time in her life and something that she continues to explore through her writing even now.

Folklore, Taylor's first pandemic album, is a mixture of fantasy and reality. One of the most coveted parts of *folklore* is the high-school trilogy that she explains involves a cast of characters named Betty, Augustine and James. 'August', 'cardigan' and 'betty' tell the story of a love triangle from each character's point of view. They're three beautiful songs, even if they didn't have a complicated fiction woven into them, but knowing they do encourages the listener to delve deeper, and the musical structure invites nostalgia, a memory box to open, back to teen life.

This trilogy ensures that the 'other woman' gets a voice too, writing any feminist wrongs of 'Better Than Revenge' by understanding that love can happen to everyone in a triangle – and that they each deserve a voice to show that hidden affairs are not always straightforward.

Incidentally, 'august' and 'betty' show us just how much attention to detail Taylor pays to her songwriting and the storytelling within it. At the 2:45 mark in 'august', we hear Augustine tell us of pulling up to pick up James in her car, cancelling her plans for the boy she loved. Concurrently, also at 2:45 in 'betty', James tells Betty of Augustine's invitation to drive in the car with her, with his own gaze and promises of never really forgetting Betty.

These two wildly different recollections of an affair are drawn together at that same moment by one common fact: that James indeed got in Augustine's car. It shows two sides of the same story. Taylor Swift doesn't need to do this when she writes music, but she gives us depth, story and validity in the telling of what young people feel and think.

We all learn these lessons throughout our young lives. What makes Taylor unique, and therefore the fan relationship with her unique too, is that we are learning them together. Taylor Swift's back catalogue is a diary of her life – the events that happened and how she felt about them – and she is helping her fans, who are so often searching for guidance, to experience and understand that growth on a deeper level, through music, speaks to us in a way that our peers can't.

The same can be said of fandom, and why it is often young people who inhabit these spaces. The time during which we develop our brains and our ideologies can be quite isolating.

Fandoms represent the things we care the most about, and when we find them it can feel like being seen for the first time.

Fandom can also shut out the noise of reality. When young people are experiencing the most formative years of life, there is also so much happening. The education system is designed so that our most intense studies fall at the height of adolescence, as our friendship groups become challenged and divided by emotional outbursts and crushes and competition. We fall in love, we experience our sexuality – and that of others – for the first time. Sometimes our family units break down, and all the while we begin to see the harder parts of the world we live in. Young people today more than ever face the scariest world that recent generations have lived in – climate change, war in Ukraine, racist attacks and hate speech online, anti-trans movements in force, policemen murdering women who are supposed to trust them. All wrapped up with a three-year-long global pandemic and some of the most disruptive and divisive political leaders sitting at the front of it all.

Does anybody care what this does to our teenagers? And when it comes to young women, does anyone have their back?

And what happens as those fans grow up, and we become the tastemakers and trendsetters for the future? There is no question that at the younger end of society we are becoming more open, more vulnerable and more opinionated. The concerns of our futures are heard more clearly. The next young generation are labelled Alpha – because of their active, clear views on how they feel the world should change and evolve. We've already talked about the reclamation of fandom – that young people are now proud to call themselves fans, to label themselves as Swifties, Directioners, Potterheads and Whovians. Perhaps this isn't just because these communities help us to feel seen, but also because

we as fans are seeing ourselves being taken seriously by the creators – and that those creators helped us steer the ship and decide what was cool.

And as for Taylor Swift? Taylor chose us, the young and the feeling. She chose giving us a voice and, above all, someone to look up to. In return, we made her stratospherically famous. We supported her and told anyone who would listen that she was indeed *the 1*, and so we turned her into an idol.

CHAPTER 7

ALL TOO WELL

What Are Parasocial Relationships?

parasocial relationships *(noun)*:
[pah-ruh-so-shuhl re-lay-shuhn-ship]

A relationship that a person imagines having
with another person whom they do not
actually know . . . This often involves a person
feeling as though they have a close, intimate
connection with someone whom they have
never met due to closely following that person
(or character) in media . . . Though parasocial
relationships are often considered common,
they may be considered unhealthy when they
become extreme enough to interfere with real-
life relationships or daily life.

(Dictionary.com)

We're all talking about parasocial relationships these days. It's a term that has long circulated in studies of celebrity and fandom, and is now being used far more frequently as a tool to understand the ever-increasing ways in how we consume celebrities, stories and seemingly one-sided relationships. People are fascinated by the parasocial relationship – defined as an imagined relationship that one person has with someone else, usually a star. This relationship has often been built by proximity via social media, especially with the rise of influencer culture.

We're not only talking about parasocial relationships – we're LIVING them.

And most of us don't even realise it! We all want to be friends with the people we see online, especially those whose lives look the same as ours, and it's clouding our judgement when it comes to who we feel close to, and how close we feel to famous people.

Now, I'm not here to tell you that having an intimate and close-feeling relationship with your favourite superstar is unhealthy, weird or concerning. We will definitely explore how and when parasocial relationships can go too far, but it's most important that if we are experiencing feelings of love that go beyond admiration and aspiration, to somebody we don't know, that we understand a little better why we feel that way, and the ways in which we can still see that person or celebrity in realistic terms.

These days, the word 'obsessed' is thrown around with casual enthusiasm and a smile on our faces. We're all obsessed with the latest trends: we're *obsessed* with your outfit; we're obsessed with the new lip product from our favourite beauty brand. To be obsessed today is not the concerning descriptor it used to be – it's cool to be into stuff. Are we playing into the hands of the brands that want us to spend cold hard cash? Are we forgetting that our celebrities are in part here to make their living from our loving them?

It seems that we don't mind – with our celebrities, we expect a little bit of politics. In fact, we're more influenced by them that ever. We'll come back to that.

So we're obsessed with our famous friends – but are the media now obsessed with us?

Lately, media outlets are talking about fandom more than ever. There are more pop culture outlets than I've ever seen, taking the form of online journalism, social media accounts, podcasts and more. Articles in *Dazed*, Refinery29, BuzzFeed and *GQ* are analysing the culture of fandom – trying to figure out what makes fans tick, and why fans behave as they do. Their top-level assessments threaten to bring back the return of the Elvis and Beatles generations – understanding fans only as screaming, mindless obsessives. There isn't a lot of interest in trying to dig deeper into the nuances of fandom, and maybe that's because the people writing about them have not lived it. At the time of writing, Refinery29 has a segment called 'fandemonium' – great punnage, though geared towards the time-told conceit that fans are hysterical first and influencers of pop culture second.

But people are curious. The huge swell of conversation around fan culture and parasocial relationships indicates this. As does the massive rise in fandom culture itself. Fandom is becoming, dare I say it, cool. The general public are looking to fan customs and costumes for inspiration.

Taylor Swift has been transformed from niche confidante of some to must-see star of many.

What does this do to our relationship with Taylor? It validates it. It creates a connection from us to her, not just her to us. We are giving her something back, and she is benefiting from us. We did that! And other people are taking notice.

Know that as I write this, from me to you as a superfan of being a fan, that I am one of you guys. I'm not particularly interested in a world where we judge fans as lesser, especially as our influence broadens. We are awesome, and we are changing the world as we know it – by supporting our idols, surely, but also by actively developing our mindsets to share the softer, kinder, more thoughtful and open ethos of the artists that make our world a better place. Many fans would proudly say they know more about Taylor Swift than their own family members – we so often understand the assignment, delve deep into our work as fan detectives, and consider our idols as people we know deeply. It can be really fun, and we know that Taylor is inviting us to do so.

But . . .

Fandom would not be fandom without the more challenging elements of it, without understanding that sometimes fandom goes too far, and the line between fan, friend and foe can be blurred and confusing. Parasocial relationships are being talked about because they exist, and because they are becoming aspirational, but also because they can be hard to understand – both by society and by ourselves.

Parasocial relationships ultimately exist around a power imbalance between two people. If we begin to feel that our relationships with our idols have bypassed celebrity–fan level, then that is when things can get hairy. Whether it's a

'Parasocial relationships are being talked about because they exist, and because they are becoming ASPIRATIONAL, but also because they can be hard to understand – both by society and by ourselves.'

TikTok creator bearing the weight of reporting into a noisy fandom, a Taylor Swift lookalike who has taken things too far, or we are truly convinced that we are friends with our favourite celebrity, the world of parasocial interactions is broader and bigger than ever before.

All of this is aided by the huge influx of media we have about celebrity life now. It is a hop, skip and a jump from a parasocial relationship to the world of gossip forums, blind items and paparazzi shots – all of these aiding our fixation on knowing as much as we can about stars, and thus enhancing our relationship and seemingly our understanding of them as people. We can literally know where a Jonas Brother (for example) is having lunch today just from opening our phones and checking their Stories, or DeuxMoi, or Reddit. We might even go eat there the next day, just to get a taste of the food they ate or the surroundings they took in. Forever looking for ways to relate, for common ground, with our stars.

When does it become an invasion of celebrity privacy? Some fans may shift into darker territory: online sleuthing may become trolling; debates with other fans turns into bullying culture. Some of us are even so upset by a celebrity's decision that we try to get them sectioned via social media campaigning. In rarer cases, people are losing their grip on what it means to be a fan so much that they are going to the extremes of physically stalking and harassing celebrities. There's a thin line between it all, and it's important to know that so often the extremes we'll uncover in this section of the book start with the best intentions.

What is obsession, *real* obsession? Why do we experience it? Are some of us more inclined to try to connect to stars and shiny people than others?

Taylor's trajectory is unique – the amount of highly connected fans she has is a phenomenon. And her fanbase is growing every day, as the hype branches out further and further. Of course she is not the only one who has a fanbase eager to share her genius with the world. Harry Styles is another star who is talked about specifically in relationship to his diehard fandom, and of course we can't leave behind the Beyhive, Gaga's Little Monsters and the BTS Army – all communities that would do almost anything to help prop up their idols.

Our fandom is intensifying as we have more access to our idols online. Is being able to see every angle of every moment of every concert on TikTok giving us *life*, or giving us mental disorders and unstable one-way connections?

Are we endangering stars? Are stars endangering us? Or are they making us better, kinder people? Are we so in touch with our feels, our connection to celebrities, that we are losing our grip on reality? Why are some of us more subject to flights of fantasy, and some of us absolutely convinced that what we feel is real? And, at the end of the day, are we doing anything *wrong*? And if we are . . . why does it feel so right?!

CHAPTER 8

I BET YOU THINK ABOUT ME

Stalkers

Since we have had celebrities, we have had fans that go too far. We've all heard about stalkers. We've all seen episodes of various US teen dramas featuring dangerous ex-boyfriends or rival frenemies that go too far with a vengeful stalking prank. The internet is rich with famous clips from *Fatal Attraction* (the origin of the term 'bunny boiler') and *The Bodyguard*. We've heard scary celebrity stalker stories passed down like urban legend from community to community, generation to generation. Stalkers sit on the outside of the shiny world of celebrity, a hard-to-understand and hard-to-imagine state of intense obsession.

How does one define a stalker, and who are the people that stalk celebrities? Why do they do it? When we talk about stalking, can we talk about trolling in the same breath? In a world where everything is online, can stalking exist online too?

Mark Duffett's brilliant book *Understanding Fandom* talks about the 'slippery slope' of being a fan – how quickly and naturally feelings can move from appreciation to admiration to obsession. As fans, we crave strong emotion and connection, especially from our idols, and sometimes it can be confusing to understand that there is a difference between a good or bad connection and feeling:

> *'Because the process of becoming a fan can involve being emotionally overwhelmed by the discovery of a powerful inner conviction, it can feel pleasantly unsettling.'*

We all know what it feels like to experience a slightly nice discomfort. It's the feeling we get from a first date, or from the exhilaration of doing something a bit dangerous or naughty like shoplifting (please don't shoplift). It's the buzz we get from sending a DM to a star on Instagram, and wondering if they'll actually ever read it. It's possible to imagine how that danger factor can start to go further than is acceptable.

Duffett continues:

> *'Fans become fascinated by realms of meaning developed by other people. Many discover emotive connections to famous individuals', and finally, quoting Fred Vermoral's STARLUST, "Fanhood can be a quite frightening kind of possession."'*

It's this possession that I want us to focus on. If you think about it, have you ever done anything as a fan that was a step too far because at the time you really thought it might increase your chances of contact, or conquest, of your idol? I think if we're honest, we all have. If that desire can possess us all, then it's not hard to imagine why some people don't understand how to moderate it.

Fandom often feels like an emotion itself rather than an active or deliberate choice.

The act of existing in the community of fandom is where we express ourselves and share our feels, but the private communion of living with our fandom is more private, more consuming.

Celebrity Worship Syndrome

Celebrity Worship Syndrome is a term that has been floating around online and in psychology circles since 2012 as a way to understand what happens to people who have deep connections to celebrities. The Celebrity Worship Scale was introduced by three psychologists, McCutcheon, Lange and Houran, in 2002. This scale was designed to help people understand the levels of celebrity worship and attachment at three different levels or stages.

Celebrity Worship Syndrome suggests there is a more official way to define our love of famous people, and offers us a scale of worship to expand on that definition:

- **stalkers** (be this of people you know or celebrities) – those who do not have the boundary in place, and actively stalk
- **specific and uncontrollable feelings** of being in love with a celebrity or a person you have never met
- **unromantic** but equally consuming notions of an intense personal connection with a celebrity
- **the more socially acceptable** – and perhaps intended – ability celebrities have and use actively to charm and capture the interest of fans or those in eyesight or earshot, to grow their fanbase and celebrity success

Is Celebrity Worship Syndrome is a real thing? Does it help you to define what you feel? Or is it just pop psychologists jumping on the bandwagon?

FluentlyForward is a celebrity gossip podcast that covers off all elements of fame and fandom, with a reflective and intellectual bent. Their dissection of various areas of celebrity is noteworthy, and I love their episode on stalkers – Shannon, the host, and her guest, Christy from *XKnowsAll* podcast, together analyse various stories of celebrity stalking.

In one episode, Shannon and Christy posit that celebrity stalking has become more accessible in recent years – of course, it predates social media and online access, but we are so much more involved in the lives of celebrities now that it is perhaps 'easier' to partake in stalking. We don't have to wait to know where celebrities are, or have been – if they're not sharing their whereabouts themselves then they are being spotted or scoped out by fans who share that information online.

We have more access than ever to the private lives of celebrities, and this can lead us to feel invited in when we're not.

The contrast today of what is legitimately accepted vs. what is stalky shows how confusing it could be to understand where to draw a line – for example, it is illegal to find out the addresses of our favourite celebrities and show up to demonstrate our admiration or hope to engage them in conversation. However, celebrities are taking to media outlets such as *Architectural Digest* and *Vogue* to give us video tours of their homes, with the aim of making them feel more within our grasp.

Shannon and Christy draw great observations as to why

 fans might take typical teenage rite-of-passage behaviour such as semi-stalking your first crush, and adapt the same strategies to find out more about our favourite celebrities. There are times in our young lives when internet sleuthing (or stalking) comes in super handy, after all, and it's not uncommon for us to consume vast amounts of information about the people we know, even the ones we keep at arm's length, just by spending a couple of hours online.

Celebrities have to deal with stalkers frequently. There are many stories – from the stalker who wanted to cut off and keep Justin Bieber's intimates to *American Idol* star Christina Grimmie, who was devastatingly murdered by her stalker at a live show in 2016.

Celebrities are never responsible for the actions their stalkers take. There are multiple shocking stories of Taylor Swift's stalkers – one who broke into her apartment while she was away and slept in her bed; a delusional male who, convinced they were in love, drove hundreds of miles to leave love letters at her door and attempted break-ins at the starlet's Rhode Island home to get closer to her.

We have recently been inundated online with content of fans in New York trying to find ways to see and meet Taylor, even if only for a moment. Where the depth of what we feel we know about Taylor via her songwriting and her persona is as it is, how do fans differentiate between the acceptable, the weird, and even going too far just for views and online notoriety?

There are viral videos orbiting social media of superfans waiting for hours outside Electric Lady Studios to get a glimpse of Taylor on her way into the studio. Many visits to Electric Lady have been set up with paparazzi, presumably by her team – we know where she is if this happens, and so, for the fans desperately keen to see her, can it be helped if they go out of their way to find her?

Swift has commented herself on the damage overexposure and fan intensity has caused her. In the *Miss Americana* documentary, she leaves her home with the film crew to a sea of paparazzi and fans waiting outside. Once safely in the car, Taylor tells the camera, 'Well, so this is my front yard . . . and I'm highly aware of the fact that is not normal.'

When a fan followed (and filmed) Taylor all the way from the studio to her private home, other members of the fandom were outraged. There is footage of her looking afraid and uncomfortable in the car as she is filmed being driven into her private garage, at her private home. Musician and record producer, and close friend of Taylor's, Jack Antonoff's wedding was another scene of hysteria – hundreds of fans waiting outside the venue to catch a glimpse of Swift, both at the rehearsal dinner and the wedding itself. Where do we draw the line? When do we decide that a celebrity's right to privacy is less important than our desire to be in their orbit?

Of course, fans online piled on to denigrate this behaviour as unacceptable, that Taylor would hate it, and that the people filming these clips simply aren't fans – they're 'fake' fans who are trying to get clout online with videos and photos.

It's a confusing boundary to understand, made more confusing by those who take these liberties calling themselves fans. If it were not confusing enough, we are being told by popular franchises and streaming services that stalking is, well . . . kind of hot.

I think I've seen this film before, and I didn't like the ending

You is a Netflix series based on the popular book by Caroline Kepnes. It has inspired a resurgence in stories about darker anti-heroes. Joe Goldberg, the lead character, is on the surface a normal, awkward guy living in New York. Hidden beneath this demeanour – expertly performed by Penn Badgley – is a monster. We watch Joe as he becomes obsessed with a girl who comes into the bookshop where he works. They date, while he watches and studies her every move, steals her underwear, manipulates her life and literally tries to kill off her friends. Spoiler alert: it doesn't end well.

While the creators and Penn Badgley have dedicated a lot of media time insisting that we the viewer must not like or root for Joe, that hasn't deterred fans from expressing a fondness for him. Many viewers have crushes on Joe, despite his disturbing behaviour – we know that it is intended to be uncomfortable and awful. However, for the show to succeed it needs to develop a fanbase, and we ultimately hear the story almost solely from his point of view, with his narrative voice tying each scene together. It becomes almost impossible not to romanticise his behaviour. It's a great, addictive show – but is it helping us to find any balance whatsoever in how we approach what is acceptable in relationships?

You is not the only media normalising or romanticising the concept of stalking. Before *You* there was *Fifty Shades of Grey*, and before that, *Twilight*. All these stories are aimed to appeal to the younger viewer, and all of them feature intense men with serious self-control issues. All of these men are also *really hot*, and all of them are shown in romantic relationships with women hoping to fix them. They all find ways to control or minimise the women they are in relationships with, but are given maladies to excuse this – Edward is a vampire, so he must act accordingly to control his urges and 'protect' Bella. Christian Grey is sexually deviant (BDSM is not a sexually deviant behaviour, but it is portrayed as such in this franchise) and must, you guessed it, act accordingly to control his urges and 'protect' Ana.

It makes sense there would be parallels – *Fifty Shades* started its life as *Twilight* fanfiction – that's right, E. L. James is one of us, a fangirl! – but it is disconcerting to see this behaviour normalised repeatedly in successful franchise after successful franchise.

Joe's behaviour is defined as unhinged and wrong – and yet still we see him falling in love, having onscreen sex and expressing relatable vulnerability. For young people, at the peak of discovering healthy behaviours around sex, love and relationships, these stories will have an impact on their decisions around what is and isn't 'normal'. When we are learning the limits of love, passion and expressing our emotions, cultural offerings such as this play a role in those limits.

There is a distance to go between media portrayals of stalking and coercion to actually acting it out. But to see stalking portrayed as a sexy kind of danger damages the perception both young women and men have about boundaries.

'To see stalking portrayed as a sexy kind of danger damages the perception both young women and men have about boundaries.'

If young people are learning to ignore the acceptable boundaries and putting their needs first, then it's no wonder that fans are confusing meeting Taylor with stalking her home. These are fans who have taken in the mixed messages that society gives us, that Netflix and celebrity gossip and social media promote as a quick hit of joy and a means to our goal. And that is when the lines blur and the status changes. That is when boundaries slip and resentment can trickle in. And this, my friends, is how trolls are born.

CHAPTER 9

BAD BLOOD

Trolls, Tattle and TMZ

Trolls. No longer just a toy with colourful hair, or a mythical bridge-dweller, trolls have become part of life online. Whether famous or not, you have likely seen, or been subjected to, trolling.

The term 'trolling' was added to the Oxford English Language Dictionary in 2006, defined in this context as:

> 'a message to a discussion group on the internet that somebody deliberately sends to make other people angry; a person who sends a message like this'.

Trolls are taking over the internet, and they vary in their behaviour. Many trolls hide behind 'egg' profile pictures or fake names, creating a hobby – or even addictive habit – of sending abusive messages online. We accept them as part of everyday life now: nobody is safe. Whether you're a celebrity, brand or young person today, you're likely to have received anonymous hate in your DMs, and trolling has even trickled into IRL bullying.

Why people troll is hard to fully understand. No doubt there's an element of 'because I can' in some instances, without much consideration or depth placed into their behaviour beyond the moment they hit send. Trolls are online bullies, and there's no sign of this part of social media slowing down.

That said, there is always a real person behind the troll. Some people who have been trolled try to better understand why someone would attack another online. Lindy West's *Shrill* recounts the moment she confronted her troll – who had been leaving abusive, fatphobic comments on her blog for months. When she meets her troll in real life, he is a teenager – a boy who has lost direction and feels he could be hateful through an anonymous platform, unable to really explain why. He is not quite the scary, deliberate and threatening monster she had envisaged: he is barely an adult.

Still, his actions had repercussions – both on Lindy and on himself, and through this portrayal in the television adaptation of her memoir, we are able to see a reflective Lindy, left slightly flat at the discovery. In real life, Lindy spoke in detail to her troll on podcast *This American Life*, learning that his behaviour stemmed from his own misery and lack of self confidence. It was easier to haunt women online than to confront his own demons.

Catfish: The TV Show is one of my truest guilty pleasures. Having watched every episode at least once, it is, on the surface, a repetitive (comfortingly so) format: hosts Nēv Schulman and Kamie Crawford help people who fear they are being catfished by their online beau.

Based on an experience that happened to Schulman, Catfish coined a new term to describe a form of romantic trolling. It also delves into the way people can behave if they are safely masked by the internet. The show often discovers reclusive, socially anxious or bullied, tormented individuals who use the internet as an outlet to process emotions they are unable to deal with in the real world. This results in catfishing. The 'big reveal' moment of *Catfish* is often the most gratifying, but the kindness with which the hosts treat the catfish – compassionately helping them to try to change – is where it is most successful.

The person behind an online troll is likely to be someone who would never put forward their comments if given the opportunity to do so in reality. Just why online anonymity brings out the worst in people is not as simple as one reason, but is often attached to some form of personal, private dissatisfaction.

That doesn't mean the impact is any less. It mystifies me that it is still so easy for people to leave hateful comments, given the repercussions it has for the victim. There are parallels to stalking – stalking comes from a deep-rooted feeling, often love turned to rage, and of trolling we could say the same. The main difference is that trolling rarely faces the same legal punishment as stalking. Why?

There is something unbelievable happening in one of the deepest corners of the internet. A hidden community of people who commit their time to anonymously joining together to expose celebrities for their behaviour – from the mundane to the malicious, this community is there, poised, waiting to take down your favourite influencers.

Welcome to Tattle.

Founded in 2018, Tattle defines itself as

'a commentary website on public business social media accounts . . . people that choose to monetise their personal life as a business and release it into the public domain'. Their description continues, 'It's an important part of a healthy, free and fair society for members of the public to have an opinion on those in a position of power and influence . . . We allow people to express their views.'

It adds,

'This is not trolling.'

Formed on the notion that 'influencer marketing is insidious', Tattle's (anonymous) founders and users insist the relationship between celebrity and follower is parasocial, and that it is proven by studies that people cannot differentiate between online influencers and regular friends – and therefore said influencers are manipulating the relationships with their fans to make money.

Tattle focuses on content creators – though it does features forums on more traditional celebrities including Taylor Swift, Britney Spears and Philip Schofield, as well as TV shows such as *Love Island* and *Strictly Come Dancing*. If there is a big celebrity scandal, Tattle's users will be all over it in minute-by-minute detail.

In the world of fame, at what point does an influencer or content creator cross into celebrity? Tattle insists that influencers are 'guarded' from criticism because of the personal nature of their posting, but that they are not deserving of the same privacy often afforded to more traditional celebrities. It is assumed that followers of influencers are somehow blinded. Tattle's unified mission seems to be to decode the 'reality' of deluded fans who cannot see the truth behind the online presences they follow devotedly.

On the surface, Tattle users are keyboard warriors, seeking retribution for normal folk who are fooled by celebrities. Looking deeper, many users are partaking in a very familiar ritual. Following every move of their chosen celeb or influencer, Tattle users are fans too, just not as we know them. They seem to know everything about their target. There are threads that go on for page after page about the same influencers and public figures – whatever you call them, they have evoked a strong response. The dedication Tattle users give to whoever they have singled out is that of the most extreme, engaged *fan*. They watch every minute of every YouTube video, every reel on TikTok. They analyze every image, post description and their followers' comments – all with the goal of proving that this person is manipulating their fans.

Tattle is not a website I would suggest visiting. It is not for the faint-hearted. But it is compelling. It sucks you in. We do not thrive as humans from constant negative input or output – but it sure is addictive.

So, are Tattlers fans by another name? I think so. Fandom as we know it tends to be dominated by positivity and adoration, but there is a negative side to that exploration: a lurking obsessiveness; a pressure involved in fandom at times. If you're not stalking someone, or actively targeting them on their platforms, you might find your outlet in expressing your intense feelings with a common-minded community. But is it okay, and is it healthy?

Being a fan is to have and share knowledge.

We fans are armed with information, and we like to make sure that our friends, families and online peers are informed in the right way, building the right story to bring longevity and authenticity to our beloved celebs. We also love being the first to know, ahead of the curve – it makes us feel useful, influential, too.

Tattle users do the same thing. The 'by the minute' compulsion to share the world of their chosen celebrity nemesis is apparent. Even better if you're first to share it. When influencers announce big life moments, Tattle forums deviate into pages of screenshots, eager to get in first, to leave their best scathing commentary along with an 'I knew it!' or 'Called it!' There's almost a ritual in doing so.

The difference between traditional fans and Tattle users is that these big moments are wrapped up in a concern for the downfall of society – a lesson to be learned about how much we let influencers and celebrities get away with. There is no cheerleading.

For those using Tattle, it does seem to be an extremely consuming hobby – the notion of obsession or compulsion exists on Tattle, and it is the same compulsion that is feeding our own fan-focused addiction to celebrity content.

The Tattle mindset is as follows: we're simply trying to be responsible; if celebrities are putting it out there, it's our obligation or right to comment on it.

One could see websites such as TMZ in much the same light. It doesn't take much of a leap to go from Tattle to TMZ, other than TMZ dresses up its trolling and information sharing in a legitimate news source structure. Perez Hilton is a similar operation. Launched around the same time, TMZ and Perez have always had similar goals, with slightly different tones. Ultimately their goal is this: celebrities are doing something, and we want to tell you about it first. True fans will always question the legitimacy and appropriateness of TMZ and Perez. They are certainly not neutral or journalistic sources, even when they are accurate or newsbreaking. These sorts of sites are right at the forefront of salacious clickbait, and represent the '90s and '00s culture in perfect low light.

The early 2000s represent a toxic wasteland of media. All bets were off when it came to celebrities and how we reported on them. Alongside Perez and TMZ, there were other sites and anonymous newsletters: Oh No They Didn't and Popbitch offered up exclusive gossip and rumour, with slightly less deliberate targeting.

If it was happening in the celebrity world, no matter how

controversial or how the information was sourced, these sites would cover it. The difference between 'news' and 'gossip' blurred constantly.

This effed-up, uncontrolled and unregulated type of reporting led to many controversies – outing gay celebrities, reporting celebrity deaths before families had even been informed, constant targeted bullying of certain young celebrities such as Britney Spears.

We have come a long way since then, but the road to fandom and online celebrity culture was first trod by some of the most controversial people in the media.

Perez

Perez Hilton launched a blog in 2004, originally called PageSixSixSix, that covered celebrity gossip and news. According to the official website, PerezHilton.com still garners over 300 million hits a month. On social media Perez still has over 6 million followers, including a presence on YouTube. He is notably absent on TikTok – from which he has been removed for violating community guidelines.

Perez was, in the early days, a celebrity PA searching for success in Hollywood. In contrast to TMZ, which sets itself up as a corporate news source with many unseen journalists,

Perez set himself up as the central point of his blog, and over the years became a character and key player in celebrity circles and gossip. Perez's notoriety grew quickly – he was one of the first online platforms to report simply on the doings and don'ts of major celebrities, and soon became a celebrity himself. If you wanted to know what was going on in Hollywood in the '00s, Perez was the guy to share it first, with no holds barred.

His content, unfiltered and unpolished, positioned Perez's hot takes on the famous as one of us. Complete with crude hand-drawn commentary and doodles done in Paint (anyone remember Paint?!), it was like gossiping with a friend. But as rival sites started to pop up, and the need to keep getting views and engagement grew, the content began to change. The fun, tongue-in-cheeky gossip became uncontrolled and desperate.

Perez himself has stated that his content went from 'bitchy to downright nasty' as it grew. The need to feed his audience meant that the content posted had to be more controversial to send more people to his channel. As Perez put himself at the front of the platform, he took the brunt of the backlash – and he went from wielding the power to cancel celebs to being cancelled himself for his actions.

Creators TikTok openly celebrated the removal of Perez from the platform. Perez now declares himself as 'hated', even going as far in a 2021 interview to pronounce that if he died tomorrow the world would celebrate. Perez's brand of 'no limits' celebrity reporting is in stark contrast to the younger generation's more thoughtful media consumption.

In a world where anyone can create content and be part of celebrity culture, fans can now create their own news.

There is no refuting that Perez took it too far. TMZ is still responsible for releasing disgusting, unfiltered content in the name of getting a celebrity exclusive. Yet we, the consumer, will eat it all up. We want to know what is happening, good and bad, and we so rarely question how that information is acquired, or its legitimacy.

Are fans who report on their idols starting to do the same? Patterns in the media will repeat themselves. Our fascination with celebrities, our fandom, makes it hard to define what is 'too far'. People are used to satisfyingly juicy celeb news. We always want more, even as we continue to love our idols. The more we can revel in their lives from a distance, the more we love (or loathe) them.

Popular commentary sites on TikTok are feeling the pressure to get content out quickly now, too. With the demand to be first to share what Taylor Swift is wearing, doing or dating, when does the emphasis on fact-checking become less of a priority than hitting 'post' first? Can we be good fans if our priority becomes winning the views and likes battle?

There are so many new ways to report on what is happening in Hollywood, as well as what influencers and idols are up to. Are we getting smarter and savvier about how we present the world of celebrity? We can learn lessons from the toxic gossip culture of Perez Hilton – and the young celebrities that endured it, such as Paris Hilton and Britney, who can now speak about the damaging impact it had on them.

But . . . we are still compelled to pull back the curtain, to see and learn more about the lives of those we admire and adore. Some of us are finding better ways to do it. Can we take on the wild world of the famous and look up at it with our fan lens on *and* keep everybody safe? With more longform options such as podcasts and YouTube, with fan-led content taking a front seat, perhaps we can find a more comfortable environment to indulge in our love of the rich and famous.

CHAPTER 10

THE LAST GREAT AMERICAN DYNASTY

From Perez to Podcasts, Blind Items and Book Clubs

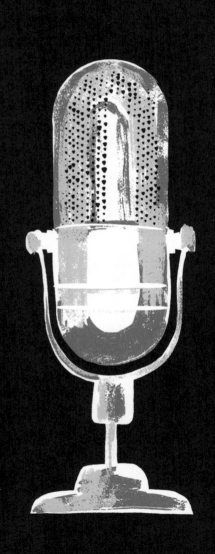

One of my favourite podcasts is *Celebrity Memoir Book Club*. Hosted by New York comedians Claire Parker and Ashley Hamilton, each week the two women sit down and review and recap celebrity memoir or autobiography. The podcast features the tomes of nostalgic 'cult' celebs – such as Mel B, Tori Spelling and Paris Hilton – or zeitgeisty reads with buzz and commentary, such as Prince Harry's *Spare*, Matthew Perry's *Friends, Lovers and the Big Terrible Thing* and *Pageboy* by Elliot Page. Then there are the 'celebrities who have no business writing a memoir', a mishmash of public figures stretching the word count with weird tips and half-baked stories – Jason Derulo and Lea Michele, I'm looking at you.

Celebrity Memoir Book Club encapsulates the joy of listening to podcasts, which can quickly publish and post, so we can all enjoy sharing celebrities as a group of fans. Having fun, friendly voices literally in your ear to help you direct and deconstruct your views about the things that matter to us is increasingly becoming an outlet for celebrity consumption. It is a lot of fun.

Podcasts have gifted us a wave of pop culture truly dedicated to being thoughtful, detailed and intricate with our gossip.

As discussed, we live in a world based around gossip, with positive and negative motivation. But for those of us who are obsessed with the world of fame – and not just the people in it, but the movement of it, how it impacts society, how it affects *us* – podcasts give us something more.

There has been an onslaught of podcasts in the last ten years – podcasts about celebrities, as we've mentioned, but also hundreds of celebrities starting their *own* podcasts, offering another supposed way for us to intimately see into their lives. We can now listen to an hour of our favourite famous person talking to us about love, marriage, parenthood, wellness, make-up, self-care, life, death and everything in between.

We have moved into a society where every element of life can be monetised and shared in exchange for validation or admiration – we simply have *so much access* to some celebrities that it's changing how we view them, and it's blurring the lines for fans and onlookers.

So, it's great to find balance, and it's great to find a podcast like *Celebrity Memoir Bookclub*. Claire and Ashley have identified that people will read into and consume what is not actually there or ever said – so their platform promises to judge celebrities based on one thing only: what they themselves have told us or committed to print in their memoirs and autobiographies.

Unlike *Celebrity Memoir Book Club*, Shannon McNamara (host of the excellent *FluentlyForward*) found her online fame in 'blind items'. Blind items are the opposite of autobiography: they are internet Owl Post, delivered quietly and mysteriously – that is, unless it's a Howler of a story – put into the world and left open to interpretation by us, the excited recipient.

Blind items are one-off written items that tell us something scandalous or unexpected about a celebrity, or the industry itself, without revealing any information. They are Easter eggs themselves, riddles with cryptic clues for the most informed of us to decipher. It's hard to know which are true and which are BS. But it doesn't really matter – that's not what we're there for. We're there to imagine what could be true, what the clues could lead to, and who might get it right first.

Shannon found that her most popular, viral moments on TikTok started in lockdown when she would share blind items about all kinds of celebrities, TV show sets or even sports stars. Shannon's warm and engaging manner gave us something to be excited about during the pandemic. We might have been locked in at home, but someone had gone to the effort to collate and interpret blind items for us, many based on viewer requests and fascinations. It's all pretty innocent, straight from the thrill of passing notes in high school, and nobody gets hurt.

When the blind items are confirmed in the mainstream media, or from the mouth of the celebrity themselves, it's another boost of serotonin – we're gleeful in our accurate guesses, victorious in our understanding of the underbelly of Hollywood.

This new wave of information – solving the mystery ourselves, crowd-sourcing the reports, is creating an online army ready to do the good work of gossip, no matter where we are in the world.

DeuxMoi

Celebrity culture could not exist today without DeuxMoi. Blind items walked so DeuxMoi could run. DeuxMoi is unquestionably the biggest celebrity gossip platform right now. It is subject to regular controversy both in the industry and amongst fans. DeuxMoi's ethos is this – if it's in the public eye, it's fair game. There is, of course, occasionally controversy around DeuxMoi, indeed including and not limited to our very own Taylor Swift. Taylor's publicist, Tree, took publicly to 'X' at the end of 2023 to refute specific comments from DeuxMoi – an extreme and unheard of act that cannot be ignored fully. The rumours that were challenged must have hit a nerve with Camp Taylor. That said, much like blind items, one might suggest that DeuxMoi is not trying to spread hate or bully celebrities. It's rather the opposite: with the lens of DeuxMoi, sharing celebrity stories is intended to be fun, escapist and constantly entertaining. It shouldn't be taken too seriously, and many of us will talk about our famous friends for as long as they are in front of us.

The pop-culture podcasts you need to listen to

1. FluentlyForward
2. Shameless
3. Celebrity Memoir Book Club
4. Sentimental Garbage
5. Unreal: A Critical History of Reality TV

DeuxMoi shares daily, to 2 million followers, the movements and activity of celebrities across the globe, utilising a dedicated fanbase of her own. This fanbase anonymously sends in sightings and spots, as well as circling rumours and fan theories, hot off the press. DeuxMoi shares all of this, and more, with neutrality. While having her own sources that are trusted and reliable, it is not often that DeuxMoi will declare something as firmly true unless it is confirmed by multiple sources. Instead, she focuses on the ifs and maybes – allowing an open forum on her channel for anyone to submit a possible piece of gossip, which she highlights with visuals to state whether she thinks it might be credible . . . or creative.

There are doubters online arguing that DeuxMoi and her fans add a new set of problems to those already set by the traditional media. We regularly – and rightly – condemn the actions and motives of the paparazzi, toting their cameras like weapons with no limits as to who they will hunt down. Yet DeuxMoi has a sort of crowdsourced paparazzi of her own, existing on any street in every city and country in the world, all through social media.

DeuxMoi's reach is huge, and more powerful and speedy than any highly paid paparazzi or photography team at this point. Two million followers can capture celebs anywhere and everywhere, for the rest of us to see.

Some see this as dangerous – Tree Paine included. By accepting this sort of media, we are not allowing celebrities even a moment of privacy. But when there are so many dangerous, cruel and profiteering outlets that exist solely to rip celebrities to shreds and make money from it, isn't it better for fans to get there first? Without seeking more than a contribution, DeuxMoi's followers hope to bring a bit of escapism to the world we live in. Ultimately, the site never deliberately tries to damage or tear down its subjects; it mostly just tells us where they eat sushi, and who they share their chopsticks with.

Admittedly, there is a tricky line to draw – why some forms of celebrity gossip are okay and others aren't. They all contribute to the same ecosystem, and we are all left wanting more regardless of how much we receive. It is important to note here that there is absolutely a line that should be drawn, and that gossip should not be limitless – medical and traumatic incidents are below that line, and it is difficult for us to understand why celebrities may respond in protest to certain gossip, and we must accept that it is their right to do so.

So, if we celebrate them as they eat their favourite pasta at Carbone, what do we do when we discover our famous friends have made a mistake, or failed to seek an opportunity to educate their many followers online? Well, while the likes of DeuxMoi and *FluentlyForward* tend to be modest in sharing harsh opinion, we fans will always hold celebrities accountable. We are so exposed to the famous. Equally, in turn, they are more exposed to us than ever, too. Their fanbases have access to their lives, their fashion, their favourite coffee blend – and increasingly so, their opinions . . . or lack thereof.

We look to celebrities more than we ever have done before, to influence us more than we ever did – fans are desperate for more content, sure, but is this part of wanting to be led, wanting to understand how to think and feel? I think so. We talk about celebrities, especially those we hold a strong bond with, such as Taylor Swift: but we all listen to them, and so what they do means more than it ever has.

Combining that with a world overflowing with conflict, developing tragedies such as climate change, culture wars and challenging the zeitgeist, there is more pressure on public figures to contribute to these conversations that mean so much to the people they influence.

We will celebrate them when they help spread the word, and we will be sure to tell them when they fuck up.

DeuxMoi

When did you start DeuxMoi?

In 2020 – right around lockdown. I had a career in fashion before this for many years. And when New York locked down, people started losing their jobs. It was a really hard time for everyone, myself included. And I needed a distraction. I had an Instagram account that had some followers and I asked them to share celebrity encounters. I'd post them, just to give everyone something to do and to occupy and distract myself. That's literally how it started. I wasn't posting news that was happening in real time – because nothing was happening.

Have you always loved celebrity gossip?

I had seen people do similar posts on Facebook – threads of people talking about meeting a celebrity and what that interaction was like. That's where I got the idea from. I would read *US Weekly* every week and watch *E! News*. I thought I knew a lot about celebrities . . . but I don't know shit compared to what these fandoms know. I'm constantly learning more and more everyday.

How has DeuxMoi developed?

When I first started, it wasn't news. It was just sharing stories – kind of like at a sleepover with your best friends. But I think that people who work in the industry discovered the account and were like, wow, this is, like, a great place to air things they've known about celebrities. Then in January 2021, when the world started getting back to normal, I received four pretty big tips – stories that I posted about before the traditional news media were able to get them out. So that's when the account took a turn and people started thinking it was a leak account or that if something is going to happen, I was going to post about it first.

Did you plan how the account would evolve?

There wasn't really any plan. I just went with the flow. I went with the information that was being sent in. So in 2021, information being sent in was no longer about old stories. It was about things that were happening right now. That's where we are right now.

Are you fan of Taylor Swift?

Yes – I like her music.

Why do you think Taylor Swift has become such a huge superstar?

The music plays a part without question, but I think the music is only part of it. I didn't have my account when she started really connecting with her fans, so I can only speak to what I've seen and read – but she invited them over her house and was interactive on social media with them. I think that drew them in. Her lyrics are relatable to people. For some reason, she has created this relationship with her fans where they think that she's like their best friend. I don't know how she did it.

Have you had negative interactions with fans?

Some fans take it too far. DeuxMoi is like a gossip column with low stakes. It's about who's dating who, who got fired from a TV show, who's going on tour. That shouldn't be things that people get that upset about, but some fans still do. But it's not that serious. It's supposed to be fun. It's supposed to be something that takes your mind off [your] own life. It's supposed to be an escape.

What do you like about fans?

They help me out. They know stuff before anyone else – and they share it with me. I appreciate it. I feel like I have a good relationship with a lot of different fandoms. They'll tell me if something I post is inaccurate, and tell me something before I even get a chance to check updates online. They are extremely helpful. I like the fandoms, I really do.

CHAPTER 11

THIS IS ME TRYING

The Politics of Taylor Swift

Being in the public eye is weird. In recent years, it has only gotten more complicated. No longer do we live in the problematic noughties, where celebrities could court controversy, say anything they wanted, break laws and hotel room ornaments and gain more fame in doing so.

We live in a world where the public, and especially the fans, want to know the viewpoint of their idols – and they want to follow suit. To understand their view on something is to understand our own.

There is much to be admired about a celebrity or public figure who puts politics and morality at the heart of their image. So what about Taylor Swift? Where does she fall in the conversation of celebrity expectation and representation? For many years, Taylor kept her politics out of sight, and only revealed her Democratic position in October 2018 – this at the time being quite a revelation after years of unconfirmed speculation about her political leanings.

It has gotten much harder in general for celebrities, influencers and, frankly, anyone with a social media account, to get this right. There is so much happening in the world, so many countering views and battle cries. There are people weighing in on everything: the proper way to show respect, sympathy, union and anger in an increasingly politicised world. If you don't know what side of the fence you're on, you might as well be on the wrong side. If you aren't representing everything, you're slacking. If you're endlessly sharing your politics, you risk accusations of being fickle and insincere.

Taylor Swift is learning about the world at the same time as she is in the public spotlight.

She is experiencing life while being asked to <u>advocate</u> for it.

And as she is deciding who she is, we are seeing more of her than ever before. Her politics aren't perfect; neither are ours. She is human, and slowly carving out a space for the things she, and we her fans, care about.

So what does Taylor care about? And what do the fans want answers on – and why?

I'd Be A Fearless Leader: entry-level feminism

It's hard work being a woman.

Taylor Swift is, at present, the most famous woman in the world. And while she is breaking records, recording music and being a role model, she is also asked to somehow be more than this. She is a fantastic role model for young women in particular. On the surface, Taylor Swift shows us that you can achieve the highest level of fame, be universally liked and be a woman.

'On the surface,
Taylor Swift shows
us that you can
achieve the highest
level of fame,
be universally liked
and be a woman.'

We can see that Taylor has learned her feminism in the public eye, over the course of the last ten or so years. A steep learning curve, feminism is often something that women learn as a requirement, a survival tool to help us through the huge imbalance of life. When we hear that there are open secrets in celebrity circles that include the most famous men sexually assaulting women and experiencing no repercussions, or women being repeatedly paid less for the same hard work, or being objectified daily by any man (or woman!) whose path we cross, feminism can be something we wield like a weapon.

Taylor Swift hasn't always been a good feminist, but I could say the same thing about me. The difference between her and us is that we can privately learn our lessons, and if we choose to share them with our peers, that is our power to wield. Taylor Swift doesn't have that choice. And so she has to decide how her feminism presents itself to the public, and to her fanbase, which is varied in both views and maturity.

That means her feminism – or at least her public projection of feminism – must be accessible. Enter: entry-level feminism.

What do we mean by entry-level feminism? Let's go back even further . . . what do we mean by feminism? It's a word bandied around regularly, especially in today's culture, but one that can have multiple meanings depending on the culture, the city, the room or even the mindset you're in.

Since the 1960s, when campaigners such as Germaine Greer and Betty Friedan began writing and advocating for women's rights, there have been successive 'waves' of feminism, with each generation focusing on different aspects of women's equality.

Author Holly Bourne describes feminism as the belief that all people should have the same rights, regardless of gender identification. In a complicated world, feminism is something that continues to develop around us – sometimes loud and upfront; often quiet, hidden so as not to disturb the wrong naysayers. Sometimes it is private, and that is okay too.

When celebrities, brands and public figures are asked today to tell us how to be politically engaged, it's likely that many of them will start, and often remain, at the beginning, with the basics: what we might call 'entry-level feminism'.

The *Barbie* movie, released in 2023, is a fantastic representation of this approach to the basics of feminism. Is a topline approach bad? No! There is room for all kinds of versions of liberation to be discussed by women. The *Barbie* movie was a cultural phenomenon with a huge marketing budget and an even bigger framework of viral content supporting it. The film itself is a mad caper that explores concepts of gender, consumerism and humanity, all while dressing Margot Robbie in iconic outfits surrounded by fun pink sets and scenery.

Barbie offers the audience an opportunity to see gender stereotypes and societal roles reversed – Kens being the submissive, second-class members of Barbieland – a world run by Barbies, by women. When Barbie, played by Margot Robbie, starts to question her role in life, the thoughts of her human owner feeding insecurity into her mind, many of the questions we ask ourselves as women in the real-world trickle into the narrative.

It considers female prettiness, male domination, the trials and hardships of the role of a woman in society. It's a great way to introduce these themes – if you're a girl who has never considered why the world is wired the way it is, *Barbie* is an important stepping stone to seeing things through a different lens.

Entry-level feminism gives us just what we need to understand why women should fight harder and have more opportunities.

It starts us off on a journey, and makes us ask the first questions about what it means to be a woman in a male-dominated society.

I'm so sick of running as fast as I can

So what about Taylor Swift? Taylor is, as mentioned, a good role model, especially for young women. She does hold some responsibility to inform her audience, and does just enough to fulfil that quotient of fame. But . . . why? Taylor is not a movie treatment written to deliberately spread a message or challenge a societal way of thinking. She is not a political movement. She is a woman – one who has been in the public eye since she was sixteen years old. Her life, though planned far in advance, is not a script. Should we expect our celebrities to be politically active, informed, vocal AND also be all-singing, all-dancing superstars?

We have, over the course of Taylor's career, seen her subjected to a certain vision of idealised girlhood and womanhood. We have seen her objectified by the media, by her fans, by critics. As we have noted earlier, Taylor was often seen as somehow less talented, less aspirational, than her peers such as Adele and Paramore, despite the similarity with which they shared stories of emotional struggles and failings in love. Could it be Taylor's 'girliness' that contributed this?

It is, even now, apparent that there are certain types of coding that society prefers women to stick to, and as such women are placed in boxes from an early age. Taylor emerged into fame as a blue-eyed beauty with long blonde curls and dainty dresses – said eyes full of wonder, excitement and innocence. That innonence and wonder, paired with a stereotypically feminine look, may be something that meant the male gaze looked over her, dismissive at best, destructive at worst.

Let's look at 'The Man'. 'The Man' marks in the sand Taylor's feelings about growing up as a woman in a misogynistic celebrity world, and is perfect entry-level feminism. The misogyny that the media portrays around Taylor has been endless – she has experienced everything – from constant speculation and reports about her love life, to red carpet interviews in which she is specifically asked who she'll be taking home with her after an event. The disdain about her credibility in her younger career is something Swift has addressed directly in a 2019 interview with Zane Lowe:

'When I was twenty-three, and people were reducing me to making slide shows of my dating life . . . and deciding that my songwriting was like a trick, rather than a skill and a craft. It's a way to take a woman who is doing her job, and succeeding at her job and making things, and . . . it's figuring out how to completely minimise that skill by taking something that everyone in their darkest moments love[s] to do, which is to slut shame . . . I don't think people understand how easy it is to infer that . . . a female artist, or a female in our industry, is doing something wrong by someone wanting love, wanting money, wanting success. Women are not allowed to want those things the way that men want those things.'

'The Man' has a clear message – it tells us:

'If I were a guy, I would be treated differently'.

This is not groundbreaking information, but this song has had young girls across the globe defiantly challenging today's reality. There is no bad side effect to that. Feminism wrapped up in a toe-tapping, upbeat track that confronts themes such as women being held to different standards in their sexuality, the highly gendered praise of being (male) 'alpha types' vs. 'scary and bossy' women and business success being so much easier for men.

Every young woman (and young man!) that hears it, and learns the words, is taking these imbalances in. If Taylor Swift helps to start you on a journey of thinking more about why it is important to fight for your corner, for your gender, sexuality, race or identity, then that is a step in the right direction.

Taylor Swift is an incredibly wealthy woman. When former radio DJ David Mueller opened a $3m lawsuit against her in 2015, she countersued. She wasn't asking for money: she was asking for truthful representation of a sexual assault she endured at his hands. She countersued Mueller for $1, a case she won, vocally speaking up about the experience she'd had – that he had groped her during a photo op, and she had lodged a complaint that resulted in his dismissal.

Swift proclaimed that she was doing this not just for herself, but also to take a stand on behalf of all women who experience sexual assault at the hands of men. She also donated £250,000 to Kesha, to enable the pop star to continue her trial against her abuser, Dr Luke, to offer financial and emotional support.

These acts that Taylor incites are lifechanging. She sets a standard and a clear moral stance when she puts herself out publicly, and it is fascinating to see when she strikes, and when she stays quiet.

You Need To Calm Down

There are many theories that circle the internet about Taylor Swift's sexuality – we will delve into that world later. But what about her output in support of queer people? Is it altruistic allyship, or is it queerbaiting, as some allude to online? Is Taylor Swift profiting from alluding to her involvement in a community she is not part of – or is she supporting LGBTQ+ fans by helping them be loud and proud?

'You Need To Calm Down' was a lead single for Swift in 2019. The accompanying music video showed Taylor in a trailer park celebrating queerness, packed to the brim with prominent queer figures such as Ellen DeGeneres, Adam Lambert, RuPaul and the *Queer Eye* cast. 'You Need To Calm Down' gives Taylor Swift fans an anthemic record in support of the queer community, though its message incorporates other personal plights – she talks about the hate she herself receives, and the hate women receive, and the hate queer people receive. There's a lot to unpack in four minutes.

The song was released to coincide with Pride 2019, and closed with a written statement from Swift to sign her petition to support the Equality Act. That petition received over 849,000 signatures. Reports also state that donations to GLAAD went up due to the release of the song.

This is all great – and Taylor's *Lover* era certainly saw her playing with demonstrating a political viewpoint that lined up with the message of the *Miss Americana* documentary. Why does she receive criticism? There are two things at play: firstly, celebrities will always receive scrutiny when showing their support for a personal cause that may not directly affect them. Secondly, it is hard to ignore that combining that support with a commercial outlet – in this instance, a single – will inevitably win you profit as well as public approval.

It is hard to recognise your own life, as a queer person, when seeing it reflected back at you loudly and proudly by a heterosexual megastar.

What affects Taylor Swift's career success in this instance also affects real people's private lives and personal moments.

Ultimately, we can assume that Taylor wanted to use her ever-growing visibility to help a community that forms a big part of her fanbase, and stake her flag in the ground as an ally (or if murmurings are to be believed, part of that community. Again, we will come back to this). But I can appreciate the uncomfortable feeling it creates, especially when these statements are often as fleeting as her Eras. Her public philanthropy and messaging sort of . . . stops once the big statement is made. Fans want more, and if Taylor puts herself in or beside that community, there may be an expectation that she will stick with it and embed herself in regular support.

But how does she do that, along with everything else?

Vigilante Shit: Taylor Swift, the businesswoman

It's a tough world for women to proudly talk about money and business.

As a fanbase, when we think about Taylor Swift, we are eager to deliver high praise around the powerhouse of a woman she is, how business savvy she is – the ruler of all she purveys. She has a hand in every decision that is made, every creative piece of work she puts out – and this is to be admired.

Sean Redmond's *Celebrity* reminds us that one of the core goals of celebrities existing around us is to make money, to bring money into society. We know that Taylor Swift's Eras Tour has literally changed the state of the economy for the better in the countries she visited – projected to generate $5 billion in consumer spending in the US alone. Our world revolves around money, and the rich are arguably richer than they've ever been: Taylor Swift included.

If Taylor is perhaps one of the richest people in the world, why do we, the mere normal folk in society, relate to her so hard?

Being a fan of Taylor Swift IS simply to KNOW Taylor. The longterm fans, those of us who have been on the journey with her up the fame ladder for over a decade, have seen her grow and learn, we've seen her fail and fuck up, we've cheered her on as she scales to new heights and cried with her as she falls to her lowest lows. Even a casual understanding of her work brings you closer to her inner thoughts than those of some of your friends or family.

And we support family, don't we? We want Taylor to keep making money so she can keep making art. That way, we get to keep experiencing it, and show our gratitude. *Take our money*, we all scream! Four editions of a vinyl that we can only order for a finite number of hours? Gimme. Hundreds of dollars on tour tickets that have us sitting in the rafters? Let me find my credit card. We're lining our wardrobes with Taylor Swift merch, and our shelves with vinyls even when we don't have record players.

'Being a fan
of Taylor Swift
IS simply to
KNOW Taylor.'

A lot of us love Taylor Swift more than we love financial security.

However, we're often happy to forget that Taylor Swift is rich. Our girl is *rich* rich. Sarah Chapelle runs the Instagram account, @taylorswiftstyled. Over 230,000 followers wait for Sarah to update us on Taylor's outfits, providing us, the fans, with the information we need to potentially buy it ourselves, or at the very least admire them.

Taylor's attendance at Jack Antonoff's May 2023 wedding was well documented. We can purchase her outfit thanks to Sarah's extensive research – but it'll set you back $40,000. To break that down: $2,000 for the dress, $800 for Gucci shoes, and, to quote our famous friend, are you ready for it? . . . *$36,000 for jewellery and accessories.* That is, plainly put, someone's annual salary. Does she look fabulous? Yes. Do we associate her with that kind of wealth? Not often enough.

Paul Théberge's essay in a July 2021 issue of *Contemporary Music Review* speaks masterfully about Taylor's politics and business acumen – including a focus on her exclusive partnership with Ticketmaster and the introduction of dynamic pricing for her *reputation* stadium tour in 2018.

Despite the extensive reading I had done to prepare for buying Eras Tour tickets, I had never understood what dynamic pricing meant – full credit to Théberge for explaining it so perfectly that I can now explain it to you, reading this book. Thank you, Paul!

Dynamic pricing is a tactic used by sellers to prevent scalpers from purchasing tickets on initial sale by rising prices and holding back a percentage of sales right up until the night of the show. Combined with using Ticketmaster's new Verified Fan platform, this would help Swift to bring her tickets to her fanbase for the *reputation* tour. This strategy would also increase Swift's own take-home sales by approximately $1.4m dollars *per show*. In stark contrast to her losing over $100m dollars in sales to resellers for her *1989* World Tour, the public's finances would suffer slightly due to this approach, but Taylor's would soar.

We also know that Taylor loves to break a record – using dynamic pricing ensured that, despite not being sold out, the *reputation* tour broke her own records for highest-grossing tour. We can see she is well on her way to breaking this record again for the Eras Tour, with 146 shows scheduled across the globe.

The Eras Tour has inspired and delighted hundreds of thousands of people. It is a phenomenon. Everybody online shares one comment:

it is worth the money, any money.

Can we put a price on what makes us happy?

Ultimately, it is important for us to remember that our idols are businesspeople. Taylor, more so than many of her famous peers, is open about this. Taylor Swift is teaching us that women can – and should! – talk about feminism and inequality and business, to aspire to make money from our pursuits and hard work. We should acknowledge that she is extremely rich, and understand why this makes her, and her life, different to ours. But to see a woman in an industry led by men fight for her right to be represented honestly, to prioritise herself and her fans, and to make business decisions at this high scale? It's important, and it's changing what young minds believe is possible.

CHAPTER 12

I DID SOMETHING BAD

Holding Celebrities Accountable, and Celebrity Anti-heroes

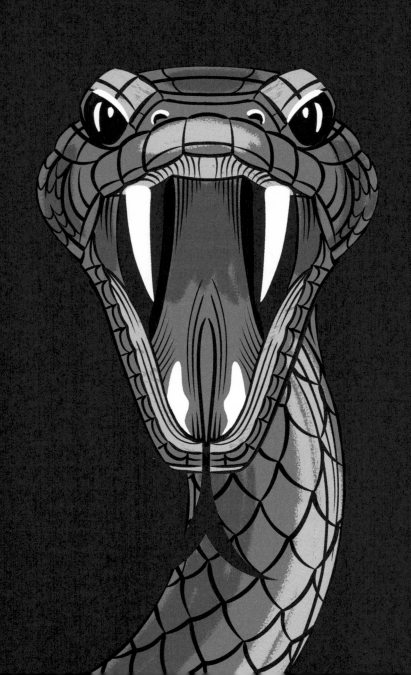

Being a celebrity comes with its responsibilities, and sometimes they get it wrong. Really wrong.

All the things we have talked about so far – feminism, queer representation, climate change and more – matter. To create a better society, we need to be able to shine a light on the problematic belief systems that still plague our world. Movements such as MeToo and Black Lives Matter have escalated quickly in the past ten years, making huge waves and gaining a groundswell of support, as well as protests and discussion around climate change, war, transphobia, body neutrality and more.

This is heavy stuff, a massive amount for any one person to take on, and social media means these fast-spread movements put pressure on us all. Celebrities form a voice of influence in our worlds, but also in our hearts, and we want them to engage with the things they care about. How do they do that without getting it wrong?

Speak Now: online platforms and accountability

There is a thin line for those with an online platform. You could be loud about the problems of the world and be told you're being sanctimonious and naggy. You could be offline for twenty-four hours and miss a huge political movement –

'Celebrities form
a voice of influence
in our worlds,
but also in our hearts,
and we want them to
engage with the things
they care about.'

and be highly criticised for not raising awareness.

On 25 May 2020, 46-year-old Black man George Floyd was murdered in Minneapolis by a white male police officer. Floyd's death was filmed and instantly went viral online, in the midst of a global pandemic. His murder set off the huge resurgence of anger that brought us the Black Lives Matter movement. People were furious, upset and afraid.

The movement marked a critically important moment in the race wars that inhabit our world, and for weeks there was a strong emphasis on focusing and raising awareness for the rights and pain of Black people. This included a social media tsunami. Celebrities, brands, people like you and me, raised their heads to pass comment or show empathy, while some stepped back to empower the voices of Black people.

For all the problems of social media, we can show gratitude for its ability to force us to wake up to some of these horrifying realities.

Many public figures and famous people got it wrong online here, but let's talk about McFly. A much-loved British pop band, McFly existed first in a world where social media accountability was not a thing. Promotion took place in print magazines, shows like *Top of the Pops*, and interactions with the public were limited to live shows and meet and greets.

Celebrating the upcoming release of their first album in ten years, McFly announced exclusive, limited-edition merch for fans just a few days after the death of George Floyd. This was met with strong criticism and backlash.

You may not think that a callous and cruel murder would have any bearing on a pop-rock band's new merch drop. McFly are much loved, and the four men who form the band are evidently good people who care about societal matters. When a misstep is made, however, there is no room for nuance or explanation. If people on social media get upset, the optics of this can trickle far beyond just the fandom. What is expected is a heartfelt apology, and if this does not happen it leaves a mark against the offender's name. The criticism McFly received was twofold: the inappropriateness of making money when the rest of the world was in grief, and the lack of thought shown in launching the drop when it could have been delayed. It's a different world to the early years of McFly's fame: fans are opinionated, and will use their voice to let their dissatisfaction be heard. There's no filter, and there is no mediator to soften the blow.

Is there something to be said, though, for keeping calm and carrying on? Selective activism is common in celebrity (in fact, it is common in all of us) – after all, it is virtually impossible to process and promote every cause. We see Taylor Swift lean into feminism, to champion women and the injustices they endure. Some public figures choose to not engage at all. This may do some damage in the immediate, but whether it impacts their profile in the longterm is often not the case. Fans of McFly still love McFly, and ultimately bought the items from the merch drop. Did those fans, or McFly, do anything wrong?

We haven't quite figured out yet what we do with that, and if *we* don't know, it's hard to know how we expect bands and their comms teams to know either.

What we do know, and have seen with 'We Need To Calm Down', is that people don't like celebrities making money in times of strife. It seems we would all rather pretend the idols we fangirl over are not doing a job. Two things can be true at the same time – celebrities can be rich *and be grateful* for their fanbase. They are human too. And humans make mistakes. So amidst all of this anger and accountability, how can we, the fans, help our favourite humans to get it right?

In Claire Dederer's book *Monsters*, she refers to 'the stain'. This 'stain' is when our beloved celebrities become marked – indeed, stained – by their actions. There are many serious examples of this: Woody Allen's films cannot be enjoyed in the same way since the sexual assault accusations made public during 2017's MeToo movement; J. K. Rowling, a once beloved and treasured children's author, has personal views that have caused huge divisiveness and upset thousands of Potter fans who grew up with her magical world. How do we, as fans, justify our fandom in these circumstances?

There is an interesting division in society. Young people are growing up in a world where there is less room for error, and judgements are cast quickly if there are wrongdoings within our celebrity spaces. There is more cancel culture than ever, the rise of which has been ever changing and experimental. We know that we want a more responsible world, with people who are more open-minded and welcoming, while also being decisive and determined to weed out the rotten members of our ecosystem.

It is a work in progress, and none of us have got it right. We are led by our fandom, and our own understanding of what we know about the idols we adore, but we are still learning to find nuance to those unfamiliar to us, or to those who tell us there is something missing from the picture.

In a zero-tolerance world, are we catching the right villains?

Bye, Sister

From the political to the . . . beauty community?

The internet is a pretty weird place, as we're learning, and so it goes that one of the most high-profile internet takedowns took place over hair vitamin gummies.

James Charles is a beauty influencer with 24 million

YouTube subscribers. In 2019, at twenty years old, James held seemingly established friendships with similarly lauded creators: Tati Westbrook, Shane Dawson, Jeffree Star – all of them creating content about the latest beauty trends, best-performing mascaras and posting 'full face of highlighter' challenges. A seemingly unproblematic community, the whole thing unravelled in the space of forty-eight hours when one link in the loyalty chain broke.

Tati posted a 45-minute video entitled 'Bye Sister', exposing James's alleged hidden dating controversies off the back of a disagreement about her own new range of hair vitamins, which James had yet to feature in favour of taking a sponsorship deal with a competitor.

What followed was madness: Tati's video also namechecked criticism of Dawson and Star, and led to all parties involved creating numerous videos, Instagram lives, tweets and clapbacks that threatened to ruin James's career. The multiple accusations, impassioned takedowns, ultimately a diversion to attempt to save their own fame, saw the whole internet watching James, Shane, Jeffree and Tati's YouTube following go down like a rollercoaster live on social media data tracking website Socialblade.

The power of fans can make or break creators and their income.

This was perhaps the first time the extremity of this was fully realised, and fans understood their power in deeming these shallow YouTubers redundant or relevant, and in doing this those creators can go broke while breaking down.

What *does* get us in a tailspin is when celebrities and icons deliberately get on the wrong side of our socially correct ethos. That makes us *mad*. But . . . those people still have their fanbases too, and, as such, a different way to unpack their acts of defiance.

Anti-Hero: reluctant celebrities and the fans who love them

Claire Dederer also tells us about another societal 'monster': the disruptors.

In 2014, a band of Manchester college friends called The 1975 got their big break. Led by frontman Matty Healy, their playful musical sound combines electronica, punk pop and '80s and '90s influences paired with tongue-in-cheek, razor-sharp songwriting. They were a bit grimy, a lot unpolished and instantly popular.

So started the rise of The 1975. They found global fame quickly. Matty Healy had the makings of a typically appealing, millennial frontman – a persuasive yet incredibly awkward energy, relatably weird, yet sort of otherworldly, angelically soft-voiced yet screamingly angry mess of contradictions. He is, above and beyond everything, dripping with stage presence, and fans eat it up – every weird, wonderful, wacky bit of him.

Now, it's not for me to write a Taylor Swift book and pretend that Matty Healy doesn't feature prominently in the Eras era. But we'll come to that later.

One thing about Matty Healy is this: he is vocal about his relationship with his fans vs. his relationship with fame. He regularly courts controversy. His relationship with fame is complicated. He and his band are musically gifted, and the lyrics they write are self-aware and politicised. Matty Healy represents the ultimate anti-hero, and he divides the internet.

'Love It If We Made It' is a song that centres on grief and rage about the current condition of society and the people who run it. The live performance is delivered complete with rageful hair pulling and is highly effective, scene setting for future generations who are inheriting a far more challenging world than Healy and his bandmates grew up in. The song makes reference to some of the biggest undoings of our society in recent years: the attitude and dangerous power of Donald Trump; the death of child refugees; the murder of Black men. The refrain at the end of verse one, 'Modernity has failed us' tells us a lot about how Matty Healy and his band feel about society and people in power today.

Similarly, in 'Being Funny In A Foreign Language', Healy apologies to seventeen-year-olds living in the world today, – an eerily moving apology for the state the world has been left in for teens today to clean up.

But . . . there is the other side to The 1975. There is everything that Swifties took objection to. There is alter ego Truman Black. There is . . . Matty Healy. We simply can't ignore these things. It wouldn't be fair for me to write about cancel culture without acknowledging that Matty Healy has a thing or two to learn about being a responsible public figure. Their stunt at the Dubai Music Festival in 2023 – already off the back of huge outcry around a recent relationship with Taylor Swift (again, I promise we will come back to this) – saw Matty Healy's Truman Black persona return from a brief hiatus in full swing to cause controversy and outcry. TikTok didn't miss a second of it.

After agreeing to appear at the festival, Healy and his band arrived on stage as if ready to perform. Instead, what followed was an insufferable, almost teacher-like lecture from Healy about the oppression of Dubai's culture. The intent, perhaps, was . . . good? We are always asking for our public figures to be defiant and take a stand against problematic belief systems. The outcome was very icky. Already on a yellow card after a wave of bad interviews, unacceptable commentary and very problematic actions, Healy's continuation to court attention via political drama turned the internet, and the event itself, sour.

Once again, we find ourselves in a difficult position – if our celebrities are not political, we're disappointed by them. If they are political, then it can spoil a fan experience in a marginalised country, or royally piss off legions of expectant naysayers who all have their own valid voice and reach.

So, what do we want? Do we want our celebs with a side of activism, or do we only want the ones we like to speak up? Do we ask that they take a stand, but only if it's the stand we want them to take?

Are celebrities allowed to be complicated? Are they allowed to fuck up?

In an interview with the *New Yorker* in May 2023, Healy was asked about the people online that are bothered by his behaviour. His (controversial) response was,

> *'If it does, you're either deluded or you are, sorry, a liar. You're either lying that you are hurt, or you're a bit mental for being hurt. It's just people going, "Oh, there's a bad thing over there, let me get as close to it as possible so you can see how good I am."'*

This quote also went viral on social media at the time of controversies being unveiled around dating Taylor Swift, and it was added to the list of wrongdoings, rubbing his new critiquers up the wrong way as if it were a direct response to their behaviour (it was an unhappy coincidence; the interview had been conducted months before).

Why do we care so much? *Are* we a bit mental?

Matty Healy has his own dedicated fanbase. What do they see that others don't? Is it the true nature of the man behind the mask? The huge contrast of the takedown tweets vs. the unwavering loyalty of his fandom is puzzling, but here's what we know: people love him, and people hate him. The people who love him have worked to understand the nuance of the 'real' Matty and, in an interesting twist, I feel that often it's the lyrics of The 1975 that – much like Taylor's – guide the fanbase to their real substance, that bring the context missing from headlines.

Do fanbases blindly support problematic people, or are they seeing the real person? Is it up to us to decipher the good in celebrities that put forward tactless acts and commentary? It is testament to the way that fandoms will dedicate as much time and resource into getting to know the person behind the band or the brand, and it is also an indicator of how fandoms can operate against one another if they intersect on uncertain terms.

Sincerity Is Scary

If you haven't yet watched Louis Theroux's BBC interview with Yungblud, you should. It's fascinating. Yungblud, for anyone as yet uninformed, is 26-year-old Dominic Harrison – a young man from Doncaster who reached almost instant fame for his highly emotive and heavy punk-indie-style music. He has a diehard fanbase and is already embarking on global tours to serve their passion for his artistry.

At the heart of Yungblud's appeal is an unfailing dedication to his fans. His relationship with the rest of fame is far less comfortable. 'Hated', a single released in September 2023, documents this in great vulnerable detail – the strain on the relationship with his family due to his openness in the media; the demands on his person as he is perceived by the public; the rollercoaster fame has taken him on at such a young age. The song also features extraordinary openness about his childhood sexual assault.

Yungblud seems to hold himself and his responsibility to his young fans to extraordinary account. With Theroux, he is shown on and off stage at shows – both high and intensely haunted by his need to show his fans not only a good time but also his complete availability to them. This is what has grown him an adoring fanbase, and it's clear he seeks acceptance not in the notion of celebrity but in the approval of the young people he feels he can aid and help.

What Yungblud is doing we have seen before – as long as there has been celebrity there have been those that go against the grain, that push against what society expects in favour of punk rebellion. Often in the name of their fans, these disruptors have paved many paths in the music industry to help the rebels in life feel seen. My Chemical Romance were icons of emo. Paramore and Avril Lavigne gave female pop punk a voice so that the likes of Billie Eilish could go further, with a 'who gives a fuck' approach to their celebrity. Billie Eilish in particular has eschewed beauty ideals to give outcasts a way to feel heard, not just seen.

What do Yungblud and Matty Healy have in common? Aside from a devotion to their fans, they share the notion that celebrity is an undesirable side effect of art.

Fame is a necessary consequence of bringing music, thoughts and ideas to an audience of likeminded people.

Disruptors like Yungblud and Healy are famous: a result of their talent, and particularly in Yungblud's case, their ability to connect to fans. Yungblud's tortured and troubled persona (that is not to say he doesn't feel those things, but he has also chosen this presentation. This is the Yungblud we see and relate to) is catnip to teens and young adults going through the same things that he sings about. His intensity of feeling, care and responsibility towards those young fans is mutually felt, amplifying the connection fans feel to him.

But Dominic Harrison is not comfortable with fame. He sits, alongside others, on the edge of cancel culture, with many lookers on (often from older generations) unable to understand why he is famous at all – and it is important that we as fans and consumers of content find a way to understand why we justify the behaviour of our idols but take down the celebrities that we don't connect with if they fuck up.

I'll leave you with this from Healy, also from the *New Yorker* interview:

'I'm not trying to make myself famous. I want to be known for what I do. But now fame is about being known for who you are. And people are complicated. If people are going to make me this famous, I'm going to make people work for it.'

Holly Bourne
(Bestselling YA Author)

Are you a Taylor Swift fan, and why?

I am! However, I didn't realise I was *such* a big fan until I went mad trying to get Eras Tour tickets (I now have three sets!). I knew I loved her music, and had lot of respect for her business genius as a self-employed, creative person – I've always had huge professional respect for her. But yeah, obviously, I'm even more of a fan than even I knew!

The key thing for me is her lyrics, and her storytelling. I think she's a genius. 1989 was my era, where I found Taylor – I remember thinking 'Blank Space' was a total banger, but also it takes this media narrative of herself, satirizes it, reclaims it and turns it into one of the biggest pop hits ever. Lyrically she has only gone from strength to strength to strength. I just think she's a genius.

What do we need to know about feminism if we've never actively engaged in it before? How do we get involved?

Feminism is beneficial to every single human being on the planet. It is a lifelong learning process. It's different for different people – but essentially, it is fighting for equality for every human being. The 'fem' part of the word addresses the fact that historically women across the globe are at a greater loss compared to men. It's about addressing the fact that women need to be able to rise up for their human rights.

How do you perceive Taylor Swift's feminism?

It's important to give historical context to Taylor's feminism journey – acknowledging she was coming of age in the noughties, which was a feminist wasteland. Everyone said there was no need for feminism. She was famous and in the public eye before the fourth wave of feminism, MeToo, Roe v Wade etc. She's not been that far behind most other women of her generation in how and when she found feminism, her learning journey that has obviously been played out on this global stage. So she has made mistakes – but like we all do. But if we say something stupid at a dinner party, that's it – Taylor says it with a huge audience. It's been interesting seeing her feminism grow and develop – 'The Man' is very entry-level, Taylor-centric, about herself and only herself, whereas 'Tolerate It' is an incredibly sophisticated feminism song about emotional abuse that is a story, not about her, but something that many women can relate to.

As an author, how hard do you think it is for fans to untangle creative output from real life? Do you think Taylor writes fictional accounts in her music?

I think they find it very hard. Even people who know you personally find it hard – and that's one of the hardest things about being a creative person – people read into your writing and personal life even if you categorically say that it is fiction. You've got to push that away in order to create otherwise you'd be too scared to write anything. The honesty of Taylor's writing is a huge inspiration for me, and I hope one of the trademarks of my writing is that I'll go to more uncomfortable parts of women's thought processes. I have to be brave to write those things, because I know that people will think it's what I think or do.

My career is on a small scale compared to Taylor, and still I find that I do it to her, and her songwriting, even though it happens to me. You can't really help it.

To write like she does, and know that a million people are going to read into it, shows such bravery.

CHAPTER 13

YOU'RE ON YOUR OWN, KID

Obscure Fandoms and Secret Ships

When I was in lockdown, I found that I desperately needed a distraction from the voice in my head proclaiming doom and gloom. Having gone from a non-stop schedule, always out and about, to being trapped at home, I asked myself: what do I do now? How will I make the days pass?

Then I remembered EA's The Sims. I was about thirteen years old when I first played The Sims, and would return to it periodically when I had fewer life commitments and more free hours. The Sims 4 is a computer game that requires hours to play in a meaningful way. It sucks up time like a Hoover. This, I decided, was perfect for my lockdown distraction. Rather than watching movies I've already seen or reading the miserable global news, I would distract myself . . . by playing The Sims.

The Sims has always offered its users a great form of escapism and creativity. When I was younger and began my first explorations into creative writing, The Sims was there for me to create whole worlds and storylines I could see on my laptop screen. You have a few ways in which to play the game. You can follow the worlds that are already there: complete with characters, pre-built houses and basic plotlines. If you're more about the optics, you might prefer to be a 'builder': creating your dream homes without limits (or within the means of a budget if you don't use cheat codes

like the rest of us) – this brings a player the format of familiar games like Rollercoaster Tycoon or Theme Hospital.

I think the way that most people play is by creating their own Sims and building storylines themselves. The Sims is built around milestones that we experience in real life: first homes, first heartbreak, first jobs, marriage, babies, death. You name it, you can live it out in The Sims. There's an abundance of expansion packs too, where players can add island worlds, pets and farm living, magical realms and more.

So I started playing again, and was totally engrossed. I was right: the hours disappeared, the misery of lockdown eased up a bit. My immersion led to further exploration. I have a fan's mindset, after all, and am all too willing to engage and be recruited into a new fan world, often as a silent lurker. If I like something, I want to know more. I want to know what other people think.

What I discovered was this: there is a *huge* Sims 4 fandom online. The fandom has not only grown rapidly with YouTube creators, Reddit forums and Twitch streams, it has managed to influence the game itself.

We know there are always interesting ways in which fandoms engage with the creator or artist they admire. What happens when it's a game, without a face fronting it? With The Sims 4 – and others in the gaming community – fans may find themselves forming that connection with the creators who share their experience of the game online. The most significant creators are on YouTube – some reaching more than 2 million followers.

2 million followers is a huge amount of people. The Sims 4 fandom is niche, well-hidden to many who wouldn't think to hunt it down, but also . . . it's not *really* a niche fandom, is it?

There are more people in the world that know nothing about The Sims fandom, and yet it is its own ecosystem operating hourly through the people engaging with it and creating content for it. Why is it that some fanbases are so underground, and what does that mean for fandoms?

Are we entering a world in which every corner of the internet can offer a unique fandom experience?

Let's look at Kayla Sims (her surname *is actually* Sims, and she is a SimsTuber). Kayla creates content online as @lilsimsie, and is only twenty-two years old. Kayla started her YouTube channel in high school, and has been growing it for six years up to 1.9million subscribers. What does she do on YouTube? She simply plays The Sims. She builds houses and partakes in a variety of build challenges set by the community. She plays legacy challenges with generation after generation of the Sims families she creates. Kayla co-invented the famous 'Not So Berry' challenge – a ten-generation objective that themes each Sim generation, to keep gameplay creative and interesting.

Kayla streams everyday on Twitch for three hours to a million followers. Her viewers are, of course, fans of The Sims 4 – but they are also fans of Kayla. They are spending hours watching her play a game they play. Wherein lies the appeal? While I was locked down and looking for that escape, watching someone play The Sims offered the ultimate escapism. Like watching TV or a movie but at the same time receiving unplanned, fun commentary from the creator, the storyteller. Storytellers such as Kayla have an ease about them, an openness and honesty, and perhaps an aspiration for fans that is similar to that of Swifties. Kayla is just like them, the players, yet she has a platform to influence, inspire and entertain. Kayla in particular is also very open about anxiety, and supporting inclusivity. She's awkward, impassioned and, like our friend, just once removed.

Clare Siobhan is a British SimsTuber married to one of gaming's biggest creators – Ali-A. Clare and Ali have more than 20 million YouTube subscribers between them and are both known for a fun, high-energy approach to gaming content. Clare plays The Sims in a different way to Kayla. Fully embracing the world of 'custom content', fanmade bolt-ons to the game, Clare's channel focuses on gameplay with realistic, human-like Sims, adding another level of immersion into the game.

Both Kayla and Clare, as well as other prominent SimsTubers such as James Turner and Deligracy, and UK creator Plumbella, are part of EA's Game Changers initiative. This is where things get really interesting. Game Changers work directly with EA to improve The Sims, and give the fans a voice as creators who are on the front line. They also get early access to new game packs and updates, and some are even creating original content for those packs.

When does the <u>line</u> between fan, influencer and salesperson stop?

The last few Sims pack releases, as a result, directly reflect what the fandom wants: an update to family life to include more realistic babies, a British-style cottagecore pack complete with cows and crochet, and a years-old plea for horses in the game finally brought to life by the Horse Ranch pack.

It is infectious to watch Kayla's passion for The Sims shine. She is high energy, clearly obsessed with the game, but also highly philanthropic. Kayla has raised millions of dollars for US children's charity St Jude via her audience. Is it unkind to suggest that there is a naivety in working so closely with EA, whose ultimate end goal is to make money; that working with them to give the fans what they want benefits the corporation and its bottom line too? EA appear to need the creator network to help continue selling the game and its many spinoff items.

The creators lead the way; they set the trends. If they tell you a pack is worth buying, that's going to directly influence fans to put money in EA's pocket. Of course, being a creator is a lucrative industry in itself – but are they leaving the fans out of pocket? Or is escapism and storytelling not something we should put a price on?

Stay Sexy, and Don't Get Murdered

While The Sims 4 fandom exists mainly in a siloed space online, there are others that break out and become mainstream, impacting cultural trends. While The Sims 4 creators are helping line the pockets of EA, some fans are turning their passions into income for themselves.

In 2016, a fascinating new community was formed. It all started with two women at a party in LA: Georgia Hardstark and Karen Kilgariff. They recall that, as the two outliers in the room, they bonded quickly over a shared love of, and deep interest in, true crime. What happened after that is phenomenal. Their podcast, *My Favourite Murder*, launched in January 2016, the concept simple – Karen and Georgia relaying a 'favourite' or fascinating murder case to one another each week.

Thousands, and then millions, of (mostly) women quickly found themselves enthralled by the stories that were being told, led by Karen and Georgia and their enthusiasm for the subject matter. The conceit of *MFM* is that it is a 'true crime comedy podcast' – combining two themes not usually matched together, something the hosts frequently point out as irony. They are adamant that they do not make light of murder cases, but they do find ways to laugh together about the darker parts of life. This candidness, along with gruesome, gripping and often unheard stories captured the fascination of many, perhaps making it more digestible. It was, much like the gossip sharing of the likes of *DeuxMoi*, in keeping with the sleepover style of storytelling – just two friends, hanging out and sharing gaspingly gruesome campfire tales.

Karen and Georgia quickly grew a fanbase (their 'fan cult') of self-proclaimed Murderinos, and before long were one of the biggest podcasts in the world – inspiring not only a slew of similar crime podcasts, but also over time changing the face of crime trends as we know it on television, streaming services, publishing and film.

Why on earth did this particular subject matter catch the interests of so many? It is, I think, another feeding of an underground interest – something that one might not have previously felt able to openly fangirl over. What does this empowerment, this validating popularity, do for a community?

A topic like true crime incites huge emotional feeling and range in a person. When we are hearing about murder, or crimes of the same status, we feel sad, and scared, and sickened. It is overwhelming. At the centre of that depth of feeling is a vulnerability, and having a community (or two figureheads that, when we are listening with our Airpods or Beats, are literally right inside our heads, as close to our own thoughts as any outsider could get) to experience that with is intense and gratifying all at once. It incites the creation of a bond, a strong feeling of shared emotion, and that leads to the formation of a huge community online.

The familiarity of the format – two hosts, the same story structure week after week – helps us to find routine in these weird hobbies and interests. We feel a sort of gratitude to the creators for helping us find similar-minded people, and become interested in their own lives.

In 2019, their book *Stay Sexy & Don't Get Murdered* (the title taken from their weekly podcast signoff, now a globally used tagline for the brand) was published – being both a dual memoir of the two podcasters and a discussion of true crime.

As well as forming bonds with Karen and Georgia, the fancult expanded into a number of spin-off communities, including a large unmoderated Facebook group that veered itself off into other interests and hobbies. Murderinos online bonded not only over true crime, but knitting, and food, and music, and their own lives. The Facebook group was ultimately closed down – unmonitored, it led to infighting and extreme hate comments. Once again, the fandom became more than the product itself; consumed by the contrasting, conflicting opinions of the people in it whose desire to share their views skewed their ability to be kind.

We still see podcasts and fan-created content setting the forecast for what's next in trending media. The power of fans grows constantly – now that fans can create their own media, they are able to build their own followings and communities, and the mainstream is following suit.

Finding our tribe and setting trends

TikTok has been an incredible uncovering of niche communities. If you love something, no matter how off the wall, TikTok has content for you. From mainstream passions like beauty and fashion, to perhaps less publicly shared passions – subjects such as ancient mythology, TractorTok, antiques and collectibles, thrifting and more – people can find their tribe and consume content about it.

Is TikTok an influence on fanbases creating and growing niche communities, or is it simply making them more visible and validated? It's certainly changing the way in which we digest content, both in quantity and depth. It's opening our minds, giving us more opportunities to discover things we didn't even know we could fall in love with.

We are no longer a generation of young people who just consume. We can create. The power of Gen-Z and the upcoming Alpha gen is that they are indeed alphas. They are bosses, independent and ingenious, thriving in a content-led world. There is so much possibility in their (literal) hands thanks to social media and smartphones. Rather than wait for the mainstream to catch on, we can create worlds of our own, just like DeuxMoi did, just like Karen and Georgia of *My Favourite Murder*, and just like SwiftTok.

Fandoms are so powerful now. In days of yesteryear, when fan interaction was in the privacy of a bedroom or in the halls of a conference centre, there was a limit to how widespread that fandom could be – a far longer route for fans to come together and experience their beloved thing en masse. That is no longer the case. Fans can band together, combine their passion and spread it into the wider world.

Fandoms all share one thing: they are communities formed by people who have something very specific in common. That something is, without question, something they love – usually the thing they love the most. Fans share a love of telling people when they love things. The goal is always to convert, hoping to gain more fans for that artist or product and expand their contact book of friends who will

'We are no longer
a generation of
young people who
just consume.

We can create.'

want to hear the latest theories, gossip and news. Of course, fandoms always have casual passers-by or droppers-in, but the ones that stick around are the ones who truly create the shape of the community. And they create well-established worlds, populated for when people like us come to discover them, just like I did with The Sims fandom.

There are readymade worlds out there for us to escape into, and legions of people who will welcome us with open arms.

And what about the Swifties? How many offshoots of the community are there – and are there outliers? If fandoms are communities, then there will always be segments of them – and that is certainly true of Taylor's fanbase. Alongside those who follow her every move, who are influenced by her politics, her fashion and her friendships – there are those who are fully committed to her love life.

But not the love life we know as it is shown to us by Taylor and her team . . . there is something else, something more underground, with a fully fledged devotion of fans who are ready to invite you in.

These are the Gaylors.

CHAPTER 14

CALL IT WHAT YOU WANT

Gaylor

Let's ask an important question: which spaces in the Taylor Swift fandom aren't universal? Which are the underground communities, the ones that sit left of centre – that are really quite happy to go about their specific subset of fandom uninterrupted?

I simply cannot write a book about Taylor Swift and fan culture without talking about Gaylor. The elephant in the room, the queer-coded fan theory, arguably a deep-cut level of fandom. It's something that remains hidden for many fans, while it is lore, sacred text, for others.

So, before we dive in, let's ask – what is Gaylor?

In simple terms, Gaylor is the fan theory that Taylor Swift is gay, or queer, based on perceived hints, clues, interviews and visual references. There is no one set rule to the Gaylor belief system – there are theories she is bi, pansexual, gay, closeted, out and proud. Some think her Easter eggs are designed to deliberately show us messages, and some believe all her boyfriends have been beards. Some don't seem to necessarily believe Taylor is definitely gay, but love to play the game and look for suggestions that she *could* be, maybe . . .

Gaylor theories have circulated for as long as the internet has had the time and capacity to analyse and speculate. There are always facets of fandom, be it Harry Potter or

Taylor Swift, Sherlock or 1D, that ask for or understand different representations from their idol or main character – it is fascinating to me that one fandom can be so diverse and wide-ranging in its interpretation of one woman. That is not to say any one fan is wrong, clowning, stanning or deluded – it is a beautiful representation of the human mind and heart that we can all direct our love and passion into different avenues, to be dedicated to a different element of one celebrity's offering.

The first time I heard about Gaylor was probably not dissimilar to the rest of you – during the 1989 Era. The 1989 Era, as we have mentioned, was Taylor's most playful, rebellious Era – a single girl in New York, Taylor had established a girl gang of hot single friends including Gigi Hagid, the Haim sisters, Cara Delevingne and Karlie Kloss. She was living the life of a normal young woman – going out partying, enjoying single life, getting wasted at gigs and enjoying New York street life. The 1989 Era is iconic for many Swifties, their entry point to Taylor. 1989 gave us Taylor's first pop album, it gave us Bleachella, it gave us sequins, mini-skirts and heart-shaped sunglasses and, perhaps, just perhaps . . . it gave us Gaylor.

At a The 1975 show in 2014, a fan uploaded a photo of Taylor and Karlie Kloss. Karlie and Taylor are situated in a balcony above the main crowd, arms locked round each other, and multiple images and videos show them glued to each other throughout the night. This particular photo is taken at such an angle that it does, really and truly, look like they are kissing. And not just girl friends kissing . . . *girlfriends* kissing.

We won't know if this fan shared this photo in an attempt to get retweets, or if it was a real fan just so genuinely shooketh and excited to get a new facet of Taylor that they took to the internet to squeal about it. We'll probably never know – but retweets it did get, and reshares. Reactions at this new revelation were all over the internet. Known in Gaylor lore as 'kissgate', this moment has been analysed to a forensic level, by fans and more recently by the media, and considered an undeniable piece of footage showing Taylor's true sexuality.

Something even more unusual happened after this: Taylor responded to it. The photo warranted this now-deleted tweet from Taylor the very same day:

> As my 25th birthday present from the media, I'd like you all to stop accusing me of dating my best friends. #thirst

This tweet drew even more attention to the situation and got even more people talking – it was actually how I first heard about Gaylor rumours. Taylor has been known to do this before and since: raise her head above the parapet on social media to quickly shut down or discredit something that angers her (see: Damon Albarn's controversial GQ interview in 2022). So why did she post about this particular image? Could it have been a defensive reflex to protect her friend – or did it attempt to hide something real or burgeoning within her that was private?

They Are The Hunters, We Are The Foxes: the women of Gaylor

LIZ HUETT – An OG fan turned backup singer, Taylor was linked with Liz in an alleged romance in 2008–09. Liz is still making music – with lyrics and music videos that may hint at a romantic link to Taylor. Liz is openly gay. Taylor and Liz are still close now, with Liz having performed and written with Taylor as recently as 2022, on *Speak Now (Taylor's Version)*.

DIANNA AGRON – Star of *Glee*, Dianna Agron is a much beloved player among Gaylor theorists. Dianna and Taylor (known as Swiftgron) were frequently spotted spending time together from 2013–14, and many detailed accounts and theories suggest songs such as 'This Love' and 'Clean' were written about their romance. Dianna is asked about the nature of her relationship with Taylor in interviews to this day.

KARLIE KLOSS – Karlie Kloss is the most discussed of Taylor's possible love interests. During the 1989 Era, Taylor and Karlie were inseparable – appearing together on stage, moving in together and doing joint magazine shoots. Often spotted holding hands, their closeness is undeniable, and there are pages online still dedicated to speculation and evidence about Kaylor. Karlie and Taylor seemed to disconnect in more recent years, with fans going wild at a reappearance of Karlie at Taylor's Eras Tour in 2023.

ZOË KRAVITZ – Zoë and Taylor were linked together most prominently in 2020, when they appeared to be in each other's highly limited COVID bubbles. Their posts during that time shared many similar Instagram captions and settings. There are lots of posts evidencing the possibility of a Toë fling, and they still spend time in the same circles.

There are many signs, moments and interviews that Gaylor believers will point to as proof or support to their conviction that Taylor Swift is queer.

Some are more plausible than others – a pink, blue and purple wig worn by Taylor and symbolising the colours of the bisexual flag in the 'You Need To Calm Down' music video; a performance at the Stonewall Uprising fiftieth anniversary, which otherwise featured only queer musicians; her commentary for the 'ME!' music video in *Miss Americana* in which she declares the inside of her mind to include:

> 'dancers, cats, gay pride! People in country western boots, I start riding a unicorn – like, everything that makes me *me*.'

A series of tweets Calvin Harris put out about their break-up included one that read (in part):

> Last year I grew a big old beard to be taken seriously by the Grammys as a producer

– a beard of course often a reference to being a straight partner for a gay man or woman to cover up their homosexuality in the media. This is particularly hard to explain away as meaningless. Harris could have been deliberately stirring the pot and adding to speculation, or enacting some sort of vengeance by alluding to a hidden truth . . . but that feels extremely below the belt if there is no validity to it.

There are subtle clues and theories, of course – just a quick search online for the Eye Theory will give you hours of persuasive deep-cut, tin-foil hat explanations of the theory revolving around the *reputation* cover featuring Karlie Kloss's eye. A red carpet dress, a vision of rainbow taffeta designed by Christian Siriano and never worn, is posited to have been Taylor's 'coming out dress' until the intended event was thwarted, and Siriano himself has added fuel to this fire with tongue-in-cheek social media posts.

However, this chapter is here for us to ask important questions – and *none* of those questions are 'Is Taylor Swift gay?'

There could be – if there isn't already – a whole book about Gaylor, to pontificate over both sides of the story and analyse the weighty evidence and campaigns that fans have produced with dedication. But to me, Gaylor isn't really just about Taylor being gay or straight or bi – it's about us, again, and why we feel that way.

The reality of Taylor's sexuality is private to her, no matter what it is.

But what would it mean for Taylor Swift to come out as queer? How many lives would it change if she were? There is much emphasis from Gaylor truthers around the importance of Taylor's queerness for the LGBTQ+ community. Why is that? Well, undoubtedly it would amount to limitless representation – Taylor's profile is huge already, and for her to be openly queer and this famous would surely make for overwhelmingly public news. Taylor is arguably one of the most influential public figures today. If she brought representation to the queer community, it would be cast worldwide.

It is clear why this is so meaningful to her queer fans, and why they find power and strength in the possibility that one day, maybe, their own idol will speak up as one of them.

As we've explored, Taylor does already speak up for the queer community – wavering between unflinchingly loud loyalty and championing with anthemic songs and public appearances proclaiming her support of her LGBTQ+ fans. Sometimes, it feels a little poorly thought out. During the Eras Tour, Taylor made a short speech to celebrate and mark Pride Month, but didn't follow this up with any other action on her social media or otherwise.

It is still more than many do, and the Gaylor community seem to note all this with tongue-in-cheek responsiveness. Their queen is, much like the rest of the fandom, seen as human and flawed, and it's okay to not be all things to all audiences. That said, if she were queer, like them, the power in seeing themselves reflected in the most famous woman in the world would hold enormous authority.

There is much written about the way that queer and female fans add homosexual layering to some of the creative outlets and celebrities they love the most. Queer fanfiction, for example, is a hugely popular segment of the creative outlet of reimagining or repurposing much-loved stories, often imagining couples that have no bearing in real life or in the shows, books, movies or bands they are inspired by.

Why do we see queer coding in worlds and public figures that matter to us? Apart from the perhaps more obvious sense that it's fun to look for clues and hints in these worlds, that might represent our own leanings – BBC's *Sherlock* is a great idea of how the writing and acting played with queer subtext – I would suggest that something more powerful in Taylor Swift's queer fandom is the way that Taylor makes us feel so connected to her is the starting point.

Lingering on *Sherlock* for a moment, it becomes clear as the series goes on that the queer coding of the two main characters increases. The Johnlock movement online was so overwhelmingly popular that it became part of the mainstream discussion – and the creators and writers of the show evidently saw and honoured that passionate sector of their fandom. To see the fantasies of the fans hinted at and playing out on our screens gave fans a thrill, regardless of whether it suited the plot or development of those characters.

Similarly, Taylor's music is deeply connective to her fanbase, so openly emotional and relatable.

As a queer fan, being able to see facets of yourself reflected back in her lyrics has the power to be deeply meaningful.

Clues of hidden love and disapproving societal judgement in her relationships are peppered throughout. To layer on that, many of those songs are linked to periods of her life in which we know she had very close relationships with women. How could it be possible that Taylor could write so beautifully and relatedly to the queer community without experiencing it herself?

There are moments of my life that Taylor reflects so perfectly in her lyrics – and many of those songs allude to things that, as far as I'm aware, she hasn't experienced. But it doesn't matter. I still feel deeply connected to her, both for the songs that have evidenced truth, and for the ones that I read into with my own interpretations that feel close to my life. The same could so easily apply to her queer fans, and that spark of possibility is all you need as a fan to feel hope, and to look deeper, to discover likeminded fans.

Speaking of evidence, Taylor's tendency towards Easter eggs and heavy hinting gives many opportunities for every fan to see more clues towards their own theories. Where queerness is often hidden in society, it makes sense that Taylor may tell us her true sexuality through the Easter eggs in which she gifts us so many other secrets, secrets often unveiled to us before those who are not so active in the fandom.

In the 'Karma' video alone, fans have found imagery that could link to queer representation: Taylor, dressed as Dorothy, walks the yellow brick road ('friend of Dorothy' is a known queer moniker). In another scene we see Taylor portrayed as the goddess Dike – the goddess of justice in Greek mythology, but we also know that 'dyke' is a common term for lesbian. Lyrical references can suggest queerness, too. 'Lavender Haze' talks about a relationship under scrutiny, and a lavender marriage 'refers to heterosexual marriages of convenience between non-heterosexual individuals' (Source: The Swaddle).

The very specific phase 'hairpin drop' from *evermore*'s 'right where you left me' is a huge arrow, if there are any. We know that Taylor's use of words is always deliberately, forensically chosen. 'Hairpin drop' is a slang term for letting people know you are gay through subtle hints, and the fact that it appears in one of Swift's most popular unreleased songs could speak volumes. To counter this, Swift has repeatedly stated that *folklore* and *evermore* are a mixture of inspiration from reality and fictionalised points of view – protecting her from any claims made. Or perhaps she is playing with her listeners, and continuing to keep their attention.

Alexandra Wormley, Graduate Student at the Department of Psychology, Arizona State University, says of the Gaylor phenomenon, 'People just wanna see themselves in her', and that the nature of Taylor's relationship with Easter eggs adds to the fascination from fans. She also speaks of the importance of not moralising Gaylor – it's not fair to say it's right or wrong, as fascinating as it is.

Either way, it's a lot of fun to consider. We are invited frequently by Taylor to read into her art – both her music and visual representations – and she has never done anything to refute the Gaylor audience who, just like the Johnlock fans, formulate a large number of her most passionate fans, dedicating hours to taking their analysis of Taylor far beyond just what is put in front of us.

I suppose we must ask ourselves: does it all matter if it never comes to anything? It is increasingly important for queer fans to see themselves reflected in the media – and the media is slowly getting better at it. But to be seen in someone as

'There's no
doubting this:

when fans are
passionate about
something, it is
boundless.

It can be a reaffirming,
joyous space.'

influential, smart and likeable as Taylor? That's more than just important; it's potentially formative. Most importantly, it helps fans find each other and bond over shared experiences. These shared experiences can create a sense of unity and inclusivity, and no doubt can both change and save lives.

If we throw hints or Easter eggs or teasers aside . . . Taylor hasn't come out. If Taylor Swift were gay, it's a part of her private life. The vast majority of Gaylors are respectful and having huge amounts of fun. It seems to have become about much more than Taylor's sexuality. The fan theories are wild and extensive, and they empower a part of the fanbase that finds great meaning and joy in being part of a community within their fandom.

After all, fandom is not just made of one kind of fan. There are millions of us, and we all hold our own deeply personal views about Taylor and her music, and how it all fits into our life. Why shouldn't we take joy from flights of fancy, and making PowerPoint presentations, and imagining that Taylor might be closer to us than even she knows?

There's no doubting this: when fans are passionate about something, it is boundless. It can be a reaffirming, joyous space.

But when something pisses them off, they are unstoppable . . .

CHAPTER 15

THIS IS WHY WE CAN'T HAVE NICE THINGS

Matty Healy and the Taylor Swift Union

On 5 May 2023 life as we know it changed. Am I exaggerating? Maybe. Life definitely changed for *me*. At least for a little while.

What happened on that fateful Friday? Taylor Swift performed her Eras show in Nashville to 80,000 fans. Her family were there, as usual, joined by various friends and VIP guests. Matty Healy was one of those guests.

Three days prior, at the final Philippines show of The 1975's 'At Their Very Best' tour, Matty Healy had, prior to performing 'About You', looked directly into the camera that fed the big screens, and mouthed three sentences: 'This song is about you. You know who you are. I love you.'

Back to 5 May – a newly single Taylor Swift looks into her own big-screen camera, before performing 'cardigan', and mouths the same three sentences. Eighteen shows deep into the tour, Taylor had never done this before. This wasn't part of her extremely polished, three-hour-long performance. No, this was a brand-new, unexpected ad lib that saw Taylor looking bashful, blushing and out of character.

This was a statement. A big fat declaration, of . . . love? For Matty Healy??

To properly tell this tale, let's track back further. Taylor Swift embarked on the US leg of her Eras Tour on 17 March

2023, kicking off in Glendale, Arizona. Fans were surprised to notice the absence of Swift's boyfriend of six years, Joe Alwyn. Rumours started circulating immediately that a break-up was either imminent or had already happened. This kind of thing really shakes up a fandom. Everyone was rattled.

Taylor's love life has always played into the Eras of Taylor through her music, but also through her activity. The past six years had been quiet, even peaceful, for fans who had accepted Joe Alwyn as her forever person, as boring as some may say he was.

Many fans still in their teens will have never experienced a single Taylor Swift. When the break-up with Joe was theorised, fans were confused. Some were cynical, some intrigued and all of us were thinking this:

if the relationship that inspired songs like 'King Of My Heart' and 'Lover' was over, then love itself might actually be dead.

As the break-up was confirmed by Taylor's trusty news source *People* magazine, we instantly shunned Joe. We screamed that he'd dimmed her shine (see: 'Bejeweled') and kept her locked in a metaphorical basement (also see:

'Bejeweled'). 'X' labelled Joe as never a worthy contender for our blondie.

We knew the break-up was real, but we still didn't know when it happened. Cue more speculation, wonderment about how Taylor could be on stage every night smiling and singing about her ex-boyfriend. There were gaps in the timeline.

Taylor's level of fame – and her credibility – had risen significantly in the six years since she had met Joe. There had been no romantic speculation since the Tom Hiddleston saga in 2016. Her industry position has changed hugely since then. No longer seen as a serial dater, Taylor and her team were able to control the narrative in the media around Joe Alwyn. It is unheard of to have to confirm a break-up at the beginning of a huge tour, one already being celebrated, shared and studied on social media to the nth degree. Throwing in a major romantic development was surely not the plan when it came to the highly planned-out Eras Tour, and we fans found ourselves able to look for hints of Taylor's emotional state every night.

The pressure for an artist here is unimaginable – and the fact that nobody had context to the break-up or its timeline means that what happened next felt even crazier.

Enter Matty Healy. Taylor and Matty had had previous associations, including dating, since 2014.

Some even credit Matty for influencing *folklore* and *evermore*; in an appearance on *The Green Room* podcast in 2019, he declared,

> 'Taylor Swift doing an acoustic record? I can't think of a record that would sell more than that. Like, Taylor Swift's intimate return to country … Taylor, if you ever want someone to help you set up the mics for your acoustic record … I'm there.'

But still, many Swifties knew almost nothing about Matty Healy, or The 1975. As far as we knew, Taylor was recovering from a break-up, busy on tour, and there were no secrets of hers that we didn't know.

When the *Sun* dropped a story that Matty and Taylor were dating, promising a big gesture of PDA between the two of them at Taylor's next concert, fandom meltdown threatened. It seemed hugely unlikely, on every level. What could be the reason? Was it a hint at a feature or collaboration, or just typically unfounded media speculation about Taylor's love life beginning again?

Well, it did happen. And it was unmissable. Taylor's declaration was wildly out of character in many ways, and predictably romantic in others. This felt truest about the moment:

some things can be faked, but that blush of new love? It was there. And it broke the internet.

I want you guys to know why I am writing a chapter about Taylor's short-lived romance with Matty Healy. The vast majority of you reading this will find him abhorrent. It is not for me to decide Healy's true character – though we have explored it in brief terms. What I do know is that over the course of the two months that this scenario played out, the fandom was uncontrollable. It was perhaps one of the most striking demonstrations of fan culture I've ever seen, with all the trappings of new technology woven into the centre of it. What was true almost didn't matter.

What matters is the unprecedented mass presentation of a parasocial response to something that could only be seen from a distance. And so we must talk about it.

It's hard to know the intent of the 'this song is about you' act. Maybe one day we will hear Taylor's version through her music, or at least some clues as to the connection the two stars had. In a world where something that happens at one show can be global, viral news an hour later, perhaps this method was a quick and effective way to announce Taylor's new beau, suggesting that all parties involved assessed that as a safe and strategic move. Perhaps it was a miscalculated act of blind love between the two.

For some days, the whimsy of it all was what seemed to charm the fanbase into allowing such a sharp left turn. Of course, the Eras Tour would continue, and we would only get our information from the paparazzi. There was minimal intersection between Swifties and 1975 naysayers – I think everyone was so shocked by what was playing out that the only focus was on what might occur next: Matty at the next show, night after night showing his face, spotted beaming and simping. Matty and Taylor together after a show, in a car headed to her home. Matty and Taylor having lunch with Jack Antonoff in an exclusive New York club. They kept feeding the news circuit, and we kept eating the crumbs that were left, desperate to understand if this was real life or Taylor's most confusing series of Easter eggs so far.

As soon as they had come in, the tides turned again dramatically. People online – trolls, fans, keyboard warriors, call them what you want – started resurfacing footage and quotes showcasing Matty Healy's far less favourable side. The first murmurings were unsubstantiated murmurings about the live shows: that he's drunk, he kisses fans on stage, he appears to do a 'Hitler salute' while performing – notably all of these things had been featured on TikTok in the weeks prior by The 1975 fans as evidence of his performance prowess, amidst praise as one of today's most energetic frontmen. The Swifties were unsure, perhaps overwhelmed by the tide of new information surfacing minute by minute. It felt days had passed since we had learned Taylor was single, and already we had a problematic boyfriend to deal with? What was happening?!

Then the bigger accusations rolled in – Matty Healy was racist, a misogynist, a drug addict, a Trump supporter. None of these accusations can be apologised away or shied from – some of the content produced during that time showcases evidence that if Healy is not these things, he has certainly behaved or made commentary to support the rumours and the tidal wave of internet rage he was met with.

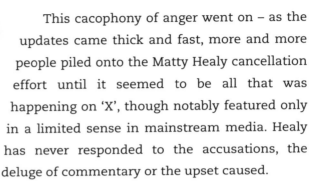

This cacophony of anger went on – as the updates came thick and fast, more and more people piled onto the Matty Healy cancellation effort until it seemed to be all that was happening on 'X', though notably featured only in a limited sense in mainstream media. Healy has never responded to the accusations, the deluge of commentary or the upset caused.

The *New Yorker* released a thinkpiece on Matty – with a lot of commentary from the man himself. The timing was all wrong, and the only piece of the article that went viral was shared by Popcrave, of Healy stating that anyone who was on the internet obsessing about him and his controversial comments needed to 'get a life'. Jaws dropped, context again removed, and the hate and anger grew.

On 20 May, at Taylor's Foxborough show, she performed surprise song 'Question . . . ?' To introduce it, she proclaimed earnestly,

'I kinda just feel like telling you . . . I've just never been this happy in my life, in all aspects of my life, ever before. I don't know, it's not just the tour. I just sort of feel like my life feels like it finally makes sense.'

At Radio 1's Big Weekend the next weekend, Matty Healy took a typically tongue-in-cheek approach when opening the show:

> 'Is it all a bit? Is it sincere? Will he ever address it? All of these questions and more will be ignored in the next hour.'

Both statements were unhelpful – fans saw Taylor's sincerity and Matty's usual glib sarcasm and understood it as a clash of intentions, or perhaps just as a loss of sanity in general. What was clear was that the fandom chose to protect Taylor even it meant that her happiness was questioned. As a result many, many attempts to eliminate Matty altogether continued to surface – social genocide through a barrage of clips and quotes.

Within a few weeks, the relationship was pronounced over – in the media, a source confirmed via *People* magazine.

What happened here? This situationship shook the fandom to its core, leading to the biggest uproar our favourite singer-songwriter has received since 2015's #TaylorSwiftisOverParty – but this time, as they say, the call was coming from inside the house.

TATTY IN TIMELINE:

17 March: The Eras Tour begins. Joe Alwyn is not in attendance

31 March: Taylor swaps 'invisible string' for 'the 1' on the setlist, sending fans into spiralling speculation

8 April: Joe Alwyn split is announced. Also, note: Matty Healy's birthday

3 May: Matty Healy mouths, 'This song is about you. You know who you are. I love you' on stage

5 May: Taylor returns in kind. Matty is in attendance, in the VIP tent

6-8 May: Matty is at the Eras Tour four consecutive nights

11 May: Matty and Taylor are spotted holding hands in NYC

12-16 May: The Matty Healy pile-on begins online

17 May: Fans launch #SpeakUpNow – an open letter asking Taylor to respond to the controversial findings about Healy

20 May: Taylor announces she is the happiest she's ever been

24 May: 'Karma' feat. Ice Spice announced

27 May: Rumours publish that Swift and Healy are 'loved up' and moving in together

1 June: A group of Swifties online propose a 'Taylor Swift fan union'

5 June: Tatty break-up is confirmed

There are major issues at the front of this mass hysteria that we should look at: firstly, did Taylor Swift make one of her first major faux pas in her career? Did she utterly misread and misunderstand her fanbase? And why do fans believe they can – or in this case, must – take such ownership of their favourite artists and, more specifically, why does it go so far when it comes to Taylor?

Taylor's fanbase is used to having some perceived agency over her actions, particularly around her public perception and her career. The fanbase, as a whole, is rarely critical. Ninety-nine per cent of the time Taylor is doing things that the fanbase wholly approve of, support and amplify – which makes the authority that we imagine we have to be validated frequently.

Taylor receives almost unfailing praise from her fanbase. She gained the mass credibility that she (and the loyal Swifties) had longed for in the media following COVID. The Joe Alwyn break-up resulted in fans supporting Swift and proclaiming to be thrilled she was finally free to shine. The thing that means the most to us is that she is happy.

Except . . . when she picks the wrong boyfriend.

There are two ways to examine this: either, Taylor made her biggest blunder and assumed that fans would support her dating anybody that made her happy, or she chose to test-run this relationship with an undeniable act, because there was a sense of trepidation. Healy is unlike any man Swift has had on her arm – his intentional lack of refinement and positively garish incitement of controversy could not be more in contrast to Alwyn. As we have said, Healy is a disruptor. In turn, it is unlike him to date someone as polished as Taylor.

TikTok creator Steven Sullivan comments insightfully on Taylor's possible mindset at the time, suggesting that Taylor perceived criticism as better public news than lingering on her heartbreak – she would rather people thought she was rebounding than think she was sad. We know Taylor cares deeply about public perception – and we can see that the quick severing and dismissal of the relationship, a remarkable backtrack, is likely a response to the huge uproar.

Confusing this situation even more was the release of 'You're Losing Me', a track from the *Midnights* vault, that seemed to directly address her anguish over Joe. We were so used to being able to interpret and appreciate Taylor's movements. Now there was nothing but confusion.

As the past years have played out, especially post-pandemic, what happens online, and what happens to our idols, has become increasingly important to our identities. Many of us spent two formative years locked in our homes – our friends as unreachable as our celebrity peers. Everything happened on our phones, on our forums, and so the playing field for what mattered most changed.

Perhaps we can no longer tell the difference between the celebrity world and our own. Taylor matters to us more than ever. And we see within her facets of ourselves. If Taylor is dating a monster, doesn't that mean we are complicit? How can we possibly allow her to make such catastrophic mistakes on our watch?

But . . . if Taylor made a human error, doesn't that make her normal? It means that she IS like us.

Frankly, we've all dated a Matty Healy – we just didn't have to make our mistakes in front of the world. But Matty Healy doesn't matter here. Yes, it is absolutely unacceptable to behave in the ways he has, whether or not it's under the guise of a persona. We know that his way of approaching public life is at best flawed and at worst harmful. In the context of being a fan of Taylor Swift, *it doesn't matter*. Because who were we mad at? Who crushed our hearts, here?

In reality, we were furious with Taylor. And how do I know this? Because when they broke up, life for The 1975 fans returned to normal. It was like nothing had happened. Matty Healy's name disappeared from the cancel culture of 'X' as quickly as it popped up. He remains unharmed.

Can the same be said for Swifties? How do we get to a point of fan culture where we possess the power to tell Taylor who she can date? Is this a step too far? The *Guardian* published an article reminding people who are readily invested in, or observing, superfan behaviour that this might not seem shocking – but honestly, it is kind of shocking. The *Guardian* refers to fans involved in this protest as 'stans'. Stans are, by definition, the obsessed, unthinking, uncritical arm of a fanbase. The fans who took against this situation were making strong judgements about what does and doesn't fit into the world of Taylor Swift. Was it deluded of them to think they had sway and authority to ask Taylor to stop dating someone she had declared love for? Well, apparently no. It wasn't.

We can't know the private reasons for Taylor and Matty's break-up. We might imagine that the pressure of the internet backlash played a role.

'Fans may now
wield a different
kind of power –
not only over other
members of the
fandom, but the
ARTIST HERSELF.'

Did Taylor choose business over love? Did she choose her <u>fans</u> over a man?

She must have understood Matty's historical controversies upon entering into the relationship, and perhaps seen something different in him – some truth behind the performer, the problematic projection.

But if the noise doesn't stop, and risked her been cancelled too – returning to a time that was traumatic for her personally, and catastrophic for her professionally, is she now forced to always choose the safer option? Isn't that kind of . . . sad?

At the end of the day the fans who created #SpeakUpNow, who asked for a fan union, may perceive it as a win. It suggests that fans may now wield a different kind of power – not only over other members of the fandom, but the artist herself.

CHAPTER 16

YOU NEED TO CALM DOWN

Fan Hierarchy

'There is one
thing about fans
and fandom that is
most important, and
that thing is this:

YOU.'

When fandoms grow, they splinter. It's safe to say the Taylor Swift fandom is a complicated place. All fandoms are varied, involving a huge group of passionate, often young people who admire, fangirl, obsess or stan on a range of levels, for a variety of reasons.

Fandoms are a funny thing, aren't they? We have explored their many elements over the course of our journey together, but there is one thing about fans and fandom that is most important, and that thing is this: you.

You, the fan, who loves the thing that you love most in the world, sometimes beyond your family, friends and pet cat. Your commitment to that thing knows endless bounds, and brings covetable joy.

Your power within a fandom is just that: POWER.

It is such a powerful thing to embrace and love and support and showcase something you feel passionately about. Not everybody feels the sense of freedom to do this, and you must never let that go. Fandom has grown more accepted over time. It is no longer a hidden hobby. It is a cool, magical thing, bringing together common-minded folk from all corners of the world.

But as they say, with great power comes great responsibility. Your fandom takes you to communities that you know will share it. Rarely is fandom experienced solo anymore. I know all too well the feeling of wanting to discover more, more, more about the film, TV series or music that I'm obsessing over – it's like feeding a hunger, and that hunger includes a desirable feeling that other people share your views, especially when the people in your direct circles don't. There is something gratifying about reading your thoughts from someone else's perspective, and that gratification is part of what creates and sustains fandoms.

It is, as we have learned, a feeling of coming together, of oneness.

The community that has been born from Taylor Swift's fandom is vast. There are always fans whose sole interest is the music, which is understandable. That itch can be satisfied by enjoying it privately, perhaps sharing it with friends who are similarly minded and going to see Taylor live – by now, after all, there are not many people who don't listen to at least some of her music. Others make it the soundtrack of their life, their only interactions with music being Taylor Swift. And from there we journey forward into intense fandom. And there is no such thing as a casual admiration there.

DeuxMoi describes Taylor Swift fans as 'innocent'. Steven Sullivan, one of the most followed Swift superfans on TikTok, describes them as 'piranhas', protecting the waters until someone slips up. Then, they strike. How's that for contrast?

Since the development of social media, fandoms can be far more expansive. There was a time, as we know, when fans simply did not have the same access to celebrities, but they also had more limited access to their fellow fans online. The development of gossip sites and celebrity magazines kept us up to speed on what our famous people were doing – so there has always been speculation – and the creation of fan forums online from as early as the 1990s helped join fans together. Fan conventions were launched as another trend, particularly in the 2000s, though they still exist today. Often created by organisations specialising in pop culture to bring fans together to meet their favourite TV or movie stars, and one another as a bonus, these events are a highly profitable venture. The likes of San Diego Comicon are now major event moments in the film and television calendar, and keep the sci-fi and fantasy fandoms well fed.

But social media means that fandoms can operate at a high frequency, high productivity level, unlimited and unregulated. This lack of regulation is where most problems occur.

SWIFTIES:
a guide (by entry point)

OGs – Been there since the beginning, fearless defenders of *Debut*. They may have discovered Swift anytime between her debut launch and *Red*'s first outing. Some are starting to raise the next generation of Swifties, and all are a walking talking encyclopaedia of the history of Taylor Swift.

1989 gen – Entering around the 2014 era, these Swifties are pop aficionados who are all about the music, and probably love Harry Styles. This fandom is still pre-TikTok, and may not be familiar with the earlier country-style albums – instead they know Taylor as strong, powerful and daring.

Rep girlies – *rep* girlies are not just a type of fangirl . . . it's a lifestyle. *Rep* girlies are masters of vengeance and retribution, empowered by Taylor's defiant return to music. Important to note there is a *rep* girlie inside all of us, but these fans will declare it a 'no skip' album to anyone who stands still long enough to hear it. *Rep* girlies are also Easter egg EXPERTS and will train the rest of the fandom to spot it all.

Lovers – the *Lover* Era started to draw in many new fans. Taylor wanted to tell the world how much she loved love and this gang loved it. Those who entered fandom at *Lover* fall into two categories: Gen-Z teens who have claimed Taylor as their own and made certain to forensically study every element of her back catalogue, and the mainstream fangirls who are in it for screaming the 'Cruel Summer' bridge together.

Folkmore intellects – for the serious, solemn Taylor Swift fan. If your entry point to TS was one of her lockdown albums, you might not have previously thought Taylor was worth a listen. *Folklore* is a conversion point for the detractors, but it's also a good opportunity for fans to embrace ennui, staying home with a candle on and pondering the meaning of life.

The Anti-heros – *Midnights* and the hype around the Eras Tour brings another slew of new bodies to the internet fandom natives, and fandom newbies. This bunch of baby fans has a lot to learn.

I rent a place in Clownelia Street

The Taylor Swift fandom is generally joined together by a couple of things: obviously, our love of Taylor, her music and her endless ambition. We also love the journeys she takes us on, including Easter eggs.

Easter eggs were once a great source of fun in the Taylor Swift world, and they still are. However they have created a competitive nature within the fandom. The desire to crack the case first becomes increasingly important and meaningful, to prove your place and knowledge as the best superfan. If you've entered into the fandom around the *Lover* Era, it has been an Easter egg *feast* since then. The fandom experience will have been defined in many ways by these Easter eggs, and the discovery of clues, hints and whispering networks of fans hoping to unravel secret information first.

So be it. If you're in fandom now, you are to become a regular resident of Clownelia Street – an internet phrase that marks a willing mind embarking on 'clowning', inspired by Swift's song 'Cornelia Street'. Clowning suggests we are open to putting on a big red fuzzy nose and falling down the rabbit hole of conspiracy and confidentiality, hunting for the many Easter eggs that Swift drops to hint at her next movement, or even a movement that is so far in the future as to presently be unimaginable. We are seeing this more and more frequently, with fans referring to sometimes years-old imagery references or lyrics to crack a future puzzle.

Taylor Swift is, as she proclaims herself on *Midnights*, a mastermind. There is an inordinate level of planning that goes into the clues she does drop, and when. It has always been evident that she gets as much glee from dropping hints as we do – it's an expression of her character that she takes as much pride in her fanbase as she does in her artistry. She wants us to be in on the secrets, but we have to work for it. And boy, do the fans work hard.

It's not even the case that fans want to be a better fan than the others – it's that they want to be the BEST FAN FOR TAYLOR, to satisfy this sense of inclusion that she has gifted us.

There are many ways to express your love as a Taylor fan – there are plenty of limited-edition records, album-branded cardigans and conversation opportunities out there – but the Easter eggs are definitely the most 'earned' way to 'win' at fandom. If you can get noticed by Taylor, that secures your position as the ultimate fan, receiving the ultimate reward.

Your entry point as a Taylor fan may have defined your role in fandom, but there are also other hierarchies at work. It goes without saying at this point that a level of intricate knowledge and detail about Taylor and her music gives you a nod of approval. If you've met Taylor, if Taylor has commented on or liked your content, you fly to higher status. If you have an inside scoop or a fan encounter, you're revered – but also sometimes doubted for your authenticity or intention.

Another way to break through into the upper echelons of the Swiftie fandom? Become a creator yourself.

There are now thousands of fans online who are making videos or writing blogs daily about Taylor Swift, and some of those creators are gaining as many followers as the celebrities themselves (although Taylor still remains untouchable, racking up over 400 million fans on social media alone).

Steven Sully, a college graduate in his early twenties, has over 250,000 followers on TikTok. Steven started his channel as a goofy comedy space, until he decided to make videos ranking Taylor's album tracks. As these started to go viral, his content veered into SwiftTok, and he hasn't looked back. Steven uploads at least once a day, sharing his thoughts and feels, reacting to music and live shows. But he veers away from news updates – stating clearly that these are risky territory if the news is unverified, or the tea is particularly hot. Treading this territory puts you at risk from the rest of the fanbase, who will be quick to cancel you if you share incorrect information, or your opinion about Taylor or her inner circle is not deemed appropriate. Ginnie Low, aka The Thrifty Swiftie, is a good example of a creator who has, unfortunately, been at the centre of accusations for getting it wrong. With 280,000 followers on TikTok, Ginnie has been challenged regularly by the fandom, accused of not fact-checking, and of stealing or copying content.

What if passion as a fan soon becomes a way to fuel other people's updates? Does it become less fun if you're constantly up for criticism? More so, if your content is helping finance your life, might you misinform your audience in order to share the scoop first? A Photoshopped image of a document crediting Harry Styles and Taylor Swift was shared all over the internet, including by reputable SwiftTok creators – all of whom received strong backlash once it was proven to be fake.

After all, nothing gets past the Swifties. We've been trained to keep a close eye.

If you've never heard Taylor Swift's music before, recording your reaction to hearing particular fan favourite tracks for the first time is a good way to gain fandom approval or clout. At present, the fandom is lauding men of the internet for falling in love with Taylor's music as we watch. YouTube creator and music producer HTHaze is one of the early initiators of this trend. He is joined now by many, curious to see what the hype is about. Their comments sections flood with gleeful Swifties thrilled to see Taylor break out of her traditional fanbase, asking these reactors to listen to more, so we can see them enjoy it for the first time.

If fans are given the power to become figureheads in a fandom, how easy is it to enact that responsibility without making a mistake? And why are some held more accountable than others? When does the fanbase draw the line?

'It's just Ashley!'

You may have come across the phrase 'It's just Ashley!'

Ashley Leechin, an American nurse and mother of two in her thirties, happens to look quite a bit like Taylor Swift. Ashley's lookalike status has, over time, become the subject of her primary content on social media, and she has amassed

more than a million followers. Her style and approach to social media has certainly changed over time, seemingly to draw in more Swifties – her hair, her dress sense, her speech intonations, and even her cat, closely follow Taylor's own.

There is no harm in being a lookalike, and lookalikes are nothing new in the celebrity world. But the Swifties often fire at Ashley, accusing her of wanting to be mistaken for Taylor, or believing she possesses some connection to Taylor. Ashley has appeared on the *Ellen* show, giggling away. Her acquired fame is clearly overwhelming to her, and addictive. In a social media 'experiment' in August 2023, Leechin worked with a YouTuber, wandering central LA with bodyguards while dressed as Taylor. This led to huge outcry from the Swifties – many fans insisting that Leechin wanted attention and was making a mockery of Taylor's own personal loss of privacy and fan hysteria. More recently, Leechin, who has always stated she is *not* a Taylor Swift impersonator, appeared at a girls' school dressed and performing as just that.

Ashley is a fascinating fan. Possessor of her own fame, her own memes and her own trolling and cancellations, Ashley is, in a way, experiencing parts of the life of a celebrity. People outside of the fandom often respond to her videos with excitement, thrilled to see someone who looks like Taylor. The Swifties, however, have had enough. They want Ashley put in her place, feeling that her act has gone too far, and may actively be hurting Taylor and her family.

Why does the fanbase turn so actively against those who do not fit their mould? There are other Taylor lookalikes on social media who do not get the same backlash. There are several content creators who do what Ginnie Lowe did – simply reporting the news as they see it. But these creators are not journalists, and so their ability to get it right all the time is not grounded in experience or training. They're just fans, trying something new, trying to stand out.

In a world where we go to social media as the primary source of news, is there also a responsibility for fans who are viewing and reading that content to know that much of it won't be verified?

Indeed, the Taylor Swift fanbase has its own set of hard-to-decipher rules alongside clear expectations that if our idol offers us so much content and material, then our job as her fanbase is to honour that. We ask a lot of Taylor Swift as fans. Endlessly, Taylor has gone above and beyond to create excitement and curiosity, to share so much of her world with us. How does she manage to give this to us, time and time again, in so many different ways?

The many faces of Taylor Swift

Taylor Swift spoke openly about the challenging concept of reinvention in the conclusion of her Netflix documentary, *Miss Americana*. Swift reflects on her level of fame:

'I wish I didn't feel like there's a better version of me out there. I feel that way all the time . . . The female artists that I know have reinvented themselves twenty times more than the male artists. They have to, or else you're out of a job. Constantly having to reinvent, constantly finding new facets of yourself that people find to be shiny. Be new to us, be young to us, but only in a new way and only in way that we want. And reinvent yourself, but only in a way that we find to be comforting, but also a challenge for you.'

While reinvention is a constant in Swift's career, becoming more curated as her fame rises, it is interesting to see her capitalise on this so specifically with the Eras Tour. A 'greatest hits' tour is nothing new to artists with long careers, and it certainly seems an exciting way to return from years of not being able to perform.

So: why the Eras Tour, and why now? Is it possible that the fans have helped to redefine something that started a challenging necessity for Swift in her twenties, into a wholeheartedly positive experience, a celebration of her artistry, in her thirties? Now, that's a real fucking legacy.

Steven Sullivan
(@STEVENSULLY1, TIKTOK)

How would you describe your TikTok?

Nonsense based on Taylor Swift. I talk about what she does, and my thoughts on it. I've built up a following where even if I didn't post my thoughts the minute something gets announced, I know that when I do get to posting them people are going to watch. For some reason I could never explain, people are interested in what I think about what she's doing.

How did you start your channel?

When I started posting I didn't set out to make a Taylor Swift fanpage. I started posting summer of 2020 – a week after Donald Trump first floated out the idea of banning TikTok. I thought: if TikTok gets banned, I don't want another social media platform to have come and gone without me using it. So, I started posting stupid videos. At some point, inspired by Dylan Mark Murphy, I made a video ranking Taylor's track one songs. It did better than what I had been posting because it was grounded in something. By the time I posted my track nine ranking it got 100,000 views. It blew up, and after that I thought maybe I could just keep posting. Three years later, here we are.

When did you first get into Taylor?

I listened to her as a kid. I loved her first three albums, but around *Red*, I stopped listening. When *reputation* came out, I vividly remember every step of that release because I just was so invested in her comeback. I was so invested in the drama. I got permission from my mom – I was still in high school – to download the album on iTunes at midnight. That was all I listened to for months. *reputation* got me into Taylor as the person she is. It got me invested in Taylor Swift.

Why are you a Taylor Swift fan?

Everything she does is so good. Even when it's not her best, it's so good. I have a very addictive personality . . . and I could feel it when it was happening with Taylor Swift. She has got me in a chokehold. I'm so fascinated by her career, and the Eras, and her progression as an artist.

What do you love about being a fan?

For me, the happier, warm side of being a fan is important. There is a lot of competition in the fandom – but I've enjoyed trying to not let myself get lost in that, and instead trying to cultivate a space where we just love her music. Finding people who are similar in that way. Going to the Eras Tour did so much for me and my faith in fandom. That whole weekend, I wasn't really online. I posted videos, but I wasn't scrolling, I wasn't watching stuff, I wasn't consuming anything. I was just sharing.

Because instead I was there physically in person with thousands of fans I got to meet and talk to and find out their favourite songs and see their incredible outfits and trade bracelets and make these connections because of this music and this person. Because it was real, because we were actually physically standing there with each other and just being . . . people. That was such an incredible experience for me. And such a nice reminder of the fact that all of the nonsense that goes on online isn't actually what makes all of this what it is. **What makes all of this is the people – this culture that evolves, and getting to be a part of that with people who I genuinely can say that I like.** I've met them through the internet and have spoken to them and gotten to know them. That is so cool and so rewarding. I really cannot put enough emphasis on how rewarding it was to get to tangibly meet people in person.

The concert at this point is more than just the show. The enjoyment I got from watching Taylor is equal to the enjoyment that I got from the six hours leading up to that – where I got to meet and interact with people who share the same interest as me in this community that exists. That's what my favourite part of all this is.

CHAPTER 17

STYLE

*The Unproblematic
Fanbase of Harry Styles*

Before the Eras Tour, there was Love On Tour.

There are montages on the internet of Harry Styles catching things on stage that have hundreds of thousands of views. Charming and entertaining to watch, just the simple act of a handsome man with great hand-eye co-ordination proves the power of Harry Styles and his unwavering charm.

I don't need to tell you who Harry Styles is. He has risen to stratospheric fame since first appearing on *The X Factor* in 2010, becoming part of boyband One Direction. We all know that One Direction went on to be so much more than that: One Direction were a phenomenon, a rite of teen passage, a way of life to so many. The heartbreak around their dissolvement was felt around the world. But then, we were given Harry Styles.

What does Harry Styles and his fanbase bring to the discussion around fans and fan culture in the context of Taylor Swift? Well, of course, let us never forget that he dated Taylor for three whole months, inspiring much of 1989. Harry remains part of the Swiftie discourse, especially when both are single and the two fandoms live peacefully side by side.

Let us travel to *Harry's House*, where fandom looks a little different to the hierarchical, complicated world of the Swifties. Harry's world is warm, inclusive and full of kindness . . . isn't it?

We know Harry Styles's origin story is completely unique to a newly digital generation. One Direction were a fledging experiment of reality talent shows, embracing social media from day one. We followed not only the formation of the band but also the development of their confidence. They were teens, and over the years we've watched them become men.

They created some of the first viral moments (Harry, upon Matt Cardle winning *X Factor*, leaned in and mouthed, 'You're going to get so much pussy' – this cheeky moment, caught on camera, was talked about by fans and media alike for *days*). This, perhaps, was the start of a fanbase that has always had existed online.

When Harry released his first single, 'Sign of the Times', in 2017, it saw him break free from One Direction without losing the fans. His artistry can be best defined as 'authentic' and 'free-spirited' – with leanings to 1970s/80s influences, Harry has carved out a niche for music that is completely 'him'. This new image, and a lot of hard work, secured Harry a stardom that most new solo artists can't count on – clever rebranding, a strong and unique identity and a very humble humanity has made Harry Styles famous arguably beyond even One Direction's success.

Of course, Harry Styles is a very good-looking man. A combination of a shy awkwardness, yet highly polished and palpable sex appeal and authority on stage means that Harry can be all things to all fans.

He is <u>innocent</u> enough for his teen fans, but <u>daring</u> enough for older admirers.

Alongside the evolution of an avant-garde, experimental fashion sense, Harry Styles truly has the full package to attract a multitude of fans.

Crying in a cool way

Harry appeared on James Corden's already viral segment of *The Late Late Show*: Carpool Karaoke, in May 2017. With 80 million views on YouTube to date, this was the ultimate piece of PR for not just a new album, but Harry himself as a fledgling solo artist. In an exchange between James and Harry, between songs, they re-enact a scene from *Titanic*, an iconic moment that defined Harry Styles. When asked if he is tearful, Harry states,

'I'm crying . . . but in a cool way.'

This was the beginning of something special. Harry Styles had defined his brand ethos, and the fans followed suit. The 'Treat People With Kindness' generation was born in that moment.

Harry's musical artistry and success has only grown. Pop bangers like 'Watermelon Sugar', 'Adore You' and 'Golden' soared. Then came 'Treat People With Kindness'. A music video with TV's hottest property at the time, *Fleabag*'s Phoebe Waller-Bridge, saw the pair enacting a co-ordinated dance routine in a dance hall. Harry, mouthing his step count as he goes, continued to charm his adoring fanbase. If Harry Styles needed to count through his steps, it was okay if we did, too.

'Treat People With Kindness' has become Harry's testimony to the world – one that the fanbase has embraced.

If Harry can be vulnerable, so can we. If Harry can demonstrate love for our planet, for our communities, for the people we interact with, the fanbase can too.

Described as *'a catalyst for radical acceptance'* by GQ, Harry Styles has this in common with Taylor Swift: while both have been making waves in the music industry, they are also changing the face of culture.

So to Harry's fandom we look. The sheer size of his fanbase combined with the respectful, warm-hearted nature of it, is an achievement in itself. Similar again to Taylor, Harry is seen both as 'king' and 'baby' – broadly contradictory but accepted and embraced by his fandom.

Harry Styles has, on the whole, avoided criticism over the years of his solo career. His fandom adores him, revels in watching his growth, and delights in celebrating his success in the form of live shows.

Love on Tour

Love On Tour, Harry Styles's epic world tour, began in September 2021. His second tour – any shows in 2020 were thwarted due to the pandemic – was ambitious, and fans were beside themselves. In contrast to a smaller 2017 tour, this time around Harry was playing massive venues such as Wembley Stadium and Madison Square Garden. Committed to seeing as many fans as possible, Love On Tour only concluded in July 2023 – meaning Harry was performing for almost two full years.

Love On Tour gave us a blissful live experience, fronted by Styles, now an iconic showman. It also gave us, as Refinery29 stated in July 2022, a fanbase that was redefining concert fashion.

There has always been precedent set for getting dressed up to go to a concert. It's part of the fun of the event, and most pop music lovers have their own pots of eco-friendly glitter stashed in their make-up drawers for such an occasion. However, Love On Tour elevated this, starting a whole new level of identity showcasing in-concert fashion.

Looking at the Love On Tour audience, we see a strongly defined sense of direction: colourful feather boas, heart-shaped sunglasses, crop tops and bell-bottoms with lively '70s prints. Glitter and sequins are a must, and shades of pink, yellow, brown and rainbow are in high concentration. Bold prints including flowers, checkerboard and waves are visible as far as the eye can see. Styles's own brand, Pleasing, adorns the fans lucky enough to purchase limited-edition T-shirts and sweaters. Merch lines follow suit. *This* is the Harry Styles look, as imagined by the fanbase.

Harry Styles has cultivated his fashion prowess over his years of growth – it has contributed largely to his ability to stand out as a must-see performer and celebrity. As his fame grew, his look became more experimental and unique, cultivating a look that plays with textures, colours and gender. There is a David Bowie vibe to it – the strong sense of self-definition, a lack of being restricted by the norms of society, a joy in redefining your style, and therefore identity, frequently.

I accessorise, therefore I am.

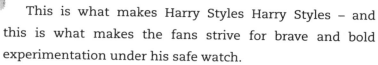

This is what makes Harry Styles Harry Styles – and this is what makes the fans strive for brave and bold experimentation under his safe watch.

Concert fashion is changing as the documentation of it on social media platforms like TikTok grows. Attendees creating their own outfits, sewing and hot-glueing and recreating what the stars are wearing, used to be in the minority. But Love On Tour felt like the origin of the takeover of creative fans, showing homage to Styles with looks that embrace all he represents. Those who weren't creating costumes were spending hours scouring fast fashion sites for the right vibes. Two things sit at the heart of this: community, with fandoms experiencing a shared vision, defining their world with a uniform of sorts.

And secondly: you can be a Harry Styles fan defined at least in part by his message of love without conditions, and go to a show like Love On Tour and feel like part of something, where you are safe to experiment and discover what makes you *you*. In doing so, you'll be supported by Harry, of course, but also by the fans who stand shoulder to shoulder with you: a kind army, radiating joy just like its frontman.

Mostly, I think these people just wanted to have a really good fucking time after years of pandemic restriction. For many young people, Love On Tour was to be their first concert, their first experience in the same room as their idol. Isn't that worth celebrating?

Love On Tour's commitment to concert style has trickled down to other post-pandemic shows – Beyoncé's Renaissance Tour has seen fans turning out amazing looks inspired by her incredible tour outfits. Of course, Taylor Swift's Eras Tour has taken on a life of its own, attendees adopting Love On Tour's expression of inclusivity and turning it into an almost battle-like need to express yourself via the many looks available from Taylor's back catalogue.

Love On Tour embodied the Harry Styles fandom. Harry Styles has fortified a safe space, himself unafraid of the trappings of what is expected of fame. Styles has grown up in the public eye, but yet has still dedicated an ethos to kindness. It's no wonder he has inspired millions of fans.

A fine line

Here's one thing I will say: Harry Styles is a man. We cannot forget the difference between being male and female in the celebrity gaze. There is a fine line, to quote Harry, between supportive fandom and inherited misogyny. We love Harry – but do we hold him accountable in the way we do female stars?

We know that Styles has almost entirely dated famous

women: Taylor Swift, Kendall Jenner, Olivia Wilde and a slew of models have all been linked to him romantically. Typically, he avoids criticism for dating celebrities – something that cannot be said for Taylor Swift, who is frequently called out for her romantic involvements.

Harry's most recent relationship with Olivia Wilde found almost all criticism sent her way. I'm aware there are fans reading this who will say that was valid. The fanbase has never really liked Wilde – she somehow never 'fit' the visual fans wanted for Harry. This only became more dramatic as the relationship lasted longer, and after the long saga of *Don't Worry Darling*'s casting woes, the two parted ways.

Harry continues to evade criticism in a way that female artists rarely do – he is praised for something as simple as walking on the correct side of the sidewalk with a date (this is decreed 'so boyfriend' of him). Fans advocate passionately for him to be allowed to have a private and personal life, while unquestionably enjoying every opportunity to see him acting as their dream man. He is rarely called to task for how politically outspoken he is or isn't – the 'treat people with kindness' ethos, coupled with on-stage support for the queer community either through supportive 'coming out' moments for fans or simply wrapping himself in a Pride flag – seem to confirm that Styles is ethically sound.

We need more Harry Styleses in our world. We need frontpeople who can confidently and experimentally rip up the rule book of societal convention. We need celebrities who will go against the grain to create emotional and physical safe spaces for their fans. Is Harry Styles afforded more of these opportunities because he is a man? He appears able to walk through fame, and the streets of London, without constant scrutiny – and has certainly gained a long-sought-out privacy after the madness of boyband life. Could we afford Taylor Swift, and female artists, the same grace?

Harry is right – we should treat people with kindness; that includes our stars and our fellow fans.

Live shows, in particular, can exemplify this with plentiful opportunities to find community and joy.

CHAPTER 18

THE BEST DAY

The Eras Tour: When Fandom Takes Over the Internet

There has never been a tour quite like the Eras Tour. The Eras Tour comes at an interesting time in Swift's career, and it's fair to say it has altered it hugely – repositioning her from famous starlet to music icon. It's an entirely unique result made of many things: the reclamation of Swift's earlier albums; the lockdown of live music during the pandemic stripping Swifties (and Taylor) of Loverfest in 2020, and the intense presence of the fandom online that made something big feel possible. And big is what we got. A show performed over the course of three hours, the Eras Tour showcases Taylor's vast stack of hits, fan favourites and deep cuts from the seventeen-year career of a thirty-three-year-old woman. The numbers seem impossible. And the demand for the show? Unparalleled.

Taylor Swift has never been more famous, but this tour presents a lot of pressure to live up to. It has sent fans into a total tailspin – tickets are more sought after than the Crown Jewels, more coveted than the shows of Taylor's most famous peers and her own past tours.

I know I tend to make it about me ...

The Eras Tour has impacted me just as much as I know it has you, reading this. Unique in so many ways, the gap between the US tour and the rest of the shows has left a chasm of want, of desperate *need*, for fans across the globe who are witnessing it night after night on TikTok. A seat at the table – or the lower bowl, or the nosebleeds – was hard won in the US, but by the time tickets went on sale overseas, it felt like going into actual battle.

The incredible demand for Eras Tour tickets means that the process is like no other – an infuriatingly admin-heavy procedure with a million steps constructed by Ticketmaster as lead vendor.

When the UK tour was announced, it was instant hysteria. My phone was buzzing hourly with friends, family and even clients messaging me to tell me. Of course I'd seen already. Every single social media app has supercharged their algorithms to show me Taylor content. I'm consuming Taylor Swift through every digital platform available to me – I listen to her music every day, I watch every fan video on TikTok . . . hey, I've even written a book about her!

I engaged in every candle emoji prayer circle, exchanging increasingly frantic voice notes with my friends, and enacting private manifestations to win a deserved place at the tour.

I received hourly queries and check-ins from friends ensuring they understood the process. Apparently I am their most Taylor-informed friend (I mean, duh). Surely helping fellow fans would all stack up to excellent karma, and I would never leave a fellow Swiftie in need.

Before long, I was persuaded to up my initial ticket budget (hahaha) to secure hospitality tickets. The stadiums that put these pricey seats up before the presale registration was over sent Swifties into tailspin. Whispers in networks, orchestrated plots to contact the stadiums directly – all so we could avoid the stress, emotion and time of possibly finding ourselves behind thousands of people in line. Every corner of the internet was abuzz.

One million people were in the queue to buy Paris tickets. ONE MILLION. We know there's a lot of us, but is it possible to imagine there are that many?

Less than two weeks prior to all of this, I had thrown my hands up, frustrated by Taylor's personal antics and the re-emergence of fandom drama, my own boundaries challenged by the controversies around her break-up with Joe and the Matty Healy drama.

Still, as the buzz built and chatter grew in my circles, my Swiftie heart *had* to have Eras tickets – my love of Taylor reignited, and the special experience of celebrating my fandom live remembered.

Cruel Summer: the Ticketmaster ticket war

Firstly, please know that if you did not get tickets to Eras, I am sorry. Your time will come, I know it.

Let's be real: gone are the days when it used to be easy and stress-free to get tour tickets. If this is your first time going to a show, trust me that it was not always this mental. Not only have ticket prices risen *substantially*, the ease with which we get our golden passes has become increasingly complicated.

What were the steps to getting Eras Tour tickets? Let me tell you.

STEP 1.

The first step was kind of under the radar. When *Midnights* was announced, you were encouraged to pre-order it to be guaranteed a code for a future tour. Keeping my fingers crossed that I might be offered the chance to try to buy tickets (!), I waited nine months: a gestation that produced the most coveted baby of Swiftie times.

STEP 2.

Tour dates. We waited months for these to be announced. Keep your eyes peeled and follow every Swiftie source available online – it could drop at any minute.

STEP 3.

Registration. This is a step I've never previously had to partake in: signing onto Ticketmaster and registering your interest via a form, entering your preferred cities, your postcode, your valid account and email address. This is when it started to feel crazy . . . what were we gearing up for, war?

STEP 4.

Then came codes. This code didn't get you tickets (four maximum, by the way). It warranted us to have an *opportunity* to *try* to get tickets. If you don't get a code, onto the waitlist you go, aka Taylor Swift tour purgatory. At this point, I'm transported back to my university applications.

STEP 5.

Code receiving day is here! Except . . . it wasn't?! So many Swifties anxiously sat, inboxes open, cursing Ticketmaster for their slowness. Didn't they know this was IMPORTANT? Then, at 4pm, we all got an an email: dates and times for the presale have *changed*. You may not receive your code, if you get it at all, for another *twelve days*. 'X' goes mad.

STEP 6.

Insert all-caps moment here: WE GOT A CODE!!!! Or, the much harder to swallow: WE ARE ON WAITLIST 😞 Now buckle in, because there are THREE presale dates, each show for each venue on sale at a different time. (I know I'm missing steps pertaining to the full *Midnights* presale process. But haven't we been through enough?!)

STEP 7.

Research. If you have the time, spend hours researching everything there is to guide success on the day of onsale: learn about the waiting room, ticket prices, stadium layouts, anything that may lend security to this random process.

STEP 8.

It's ONSALE DAY. Get in the waiting room, watch your queue number go down or a progress bar inch forward . . . then *GO GO GO*.

STEP 9.

TICKETS ARE MINE! Or . . . if you don't succeed, try again. And again. Out of luck with Wembley? How about a trip to Poland, or Vienna? Mexico is lovely in September.

After all this, I hope you were one of the Lucky Ones.

If you were, you are now invited to enter the world of the Eras Tour – with its growing list of fan-created rules and recommendations, outfit planning, surprise songs and more.

Taylor Swift takes fans through a veritable whirlwind of hits – a goosebump-inducing introduction tells us, 'It's been a long time coming . . .' (We agree) Taylor takes us through her decades of transformational music: the golden early years of *Fearless*, the snake-adorned *reputation* era, the haunting intimacy of *folkmore*, and more. It is an intimate experience and a viral sensation.

Eras Tour hashtags on TikTok have more than 25 billion views.

This tour has an online audience footprint like no other before it. Why?

The TikTokification of live music

It is undeniable that TikTok has forever changed live music. In the current cultural climate, the rules of performance are shifting daily.

If we think back to live music pre-COVID, it would be hard

to imagine that you could simply watch your favourite live show in tens of clips on social media. If you do miss out on those tickets, you can load up your FYP and experience hours of Eras Tour footage: Ultra HD close-up videos of Swift's performances from every imaginable angle accompanied by awed comments demanding to know,

'What did you film this with? Your EYES?'

Taylor has form across her live tours for creating surprises – whether that's bringing out her famous friends (Ed Sheeran, Haim, Paramore, among others) to share a performance with her, or a whimsical cover of a song written in the city she is playing. On the Eras Tour we have been gifted 'surprise songs' in which Taylor selects two songs each evening from her extensive back catalogue to perform acoustically.

The surprise songs are the subject of thousands of posts online, with fans drawing up spreadsheets to anxiously document performances before their own show. Knowing that all her songs are hugely beloved, this is a clever vehicle for Swift to represent as many of them on the tour as possible, as well ensuring each show is a unique experience for fans.

But the most interesting part is the scrutiny given to each song, perhaps to somehow understand Swift better. This only intensified after the break-up of Taylor and Joe Alwyn.

Thanks to the timing of the Eras Tour, we were privy

to witnessing Swift's heartbreak night after night, as it happened. The surprise songs turned from a fun guessing game with fans crossing their fingers for their favourite, to a game of looking for sad clues as to Taylor's state of mind. Pairing together heartbreak songs such as 'Begin Again' and 'Cold As You' on one night led TikTok to overflow with comments: 'Joe, what did you DO?!'

Each lyric, each facial expression, each inflection can be seen and examined online. A performance of 'I Don't Wanna Live Forever' (notably with no spoken introduction from Taylor), took a rapt audience by surprise, not aware that soundtrack songs were on the table. On TikTok, 4 million people watched a clip of a tearful, pained Swift, wondering aloud, with us, if she'd lost the love of her life.

This clip was instantly viral, adding to the mythology of Swift and the intimate personal connection we all feel to her. It is unprecedented to know that an artist is reliving a recent break-up with us live on stage, and redefines the long-existing narrative that the private details of her love life are no longer just hinted at in subtle lyrics or stolen moments in paparazzi shots. No, now she can tell us directly through her choice of surprise songs.

We don't know if the surprise songs are picked in advance or if Taylor decides on the night what she is drawn to. If it's the latter, in the case of I 'Don't Wanna Live Forever', and other heartbreaks chosen close to the Alwyn break-up, then we are seeing something brutally vulnerable and authentic – which we have always been promised by Swift. The Eras Tour has become, seemingly by accident, a platform to enhance the bond we share with her, and the access we have to her life.

I can still make the whole place shimmer

The 'always being recorded' nature of TikTok has led to a new phenomenon among fans, both for the Eras Tour and for others including Beyoncé, Harry Styles and The 1975 – the almost obsessive documentation of artists' tour outfits.

There has always been a cultural obsession with clothing. We have been heavily influenced by what celebrities and public figures are wearing since way before TikTok – and as per Harry Styles's Love On Tour, we want to emulate and honour the love of our famous friends by dressing to impress.

But Taylor Swift's Eras Tour offered up the opportunity for her to play with *ten* different lookbooks. She glows in gold for the *Fearless*. She shimmies in her iconic two-piece in the 1989 set, then ethereal in flowing, bell-sleeved *folklore* dresses before finally sauntering on in a dark-blue bedazzled bodysuit for the closing *Midnights* set.

Taylor has a selection of her costumes on rotation – presumably for practical reasons as well as being undoubtedly designed to bring variety to photos and videos taken by attendees to mark the different nights for media photography and social media posts. But the fandom online has taken this variety of costumes as a personal gift, marking every precious new visual with dedicated videos, spending upwards of five minutes discussing different shades of sparkle, different colours and, again, of course, possible Easter eggs.

In the first weeks of the tour, Taylor's 22 T-shirt became the focus of much examination. With three different messages that included:

It doesn't end there – certain letters were marked out in red. For completists' sakes, these letters were: **A LOT**, **EW** and **NEVER EVER**.

Surely Taylor was just emphasising key phrases for effect, right? Nope. Fans were convinced Taylor was sending a message: but what was it? Would the red letters change every night? Was she trying to tell us that a new album was coming? Was it *Speak Now, (Taylor's Version)*? Hundreds of videos played Swiftie 'hangman', showcasing what we had already and what was perhaps to come:

__EA_ NOW TA_LORS VER___N

It was a compelling case – we only needed six letters to complete our tour T-shirt Easter egg puzzle! Did those six letters ever come? No. Were they meant to, and there was a wardrobe malfunction? We'll never know. Did this clowning, this pursuit for evidence in red letters that went on for weeks ever conclude? It did not. The biggest question, though . . . does it matter? The fun of the chase is satisfying enough – and if fans ever solved the mystery of those T-shirts, it has happened after this book went to press.

Incidentally, *Speak Now (Taylor's Version)* was announced as part of the tour, an epic moment that saw her outfits turn purple in honour, gifting another reason for fans to be enthralled. It is always possible in the Taylor Swift multiverse that the Easter eggs are real – and Swift can rely on her fans to find and celebrate them.

In addition to games of hide-and-seek with tour outfits,

there is content to be found in new outfits. Fans went wild for a new sage-green dress with stunning lace cut-out in the *evermore* set. It has never been so important to be well-dressed on tour as a performer – if you can provide your fans with something as simple as a bonus outfit, it will be discussed online for days. This word-of-mouth media all generates buzz, a need to attend the tour personally and see it for yourself. The compulsion to engage with the Eras Tour on every level has seen fans paying thousands of dollars for last-minute tickets, or even to partake in 'Taylor-gating' – standing in the parking lot to experience the show from afar.

The financial separation between star and fan has never been clearer than when we explore the specifics of the Eras Tour outfits. Taylor Swift has retained such a strong sense of sisterhood with her fandom – the more famous she grows, the more her life is different to the fans who love her. Taylor is good at disguising her extreme wealth – we only see her private life in glimpses, with Swift often opting for casual, unfussy clothes outside of red carpets.

Her tour outfits are presented in similar fashion – beautiful though they are, it is impossible to interpret their value. The first hint at an upgrade to Swift's tour wardrobe was the flash of red on each boot sole – the trademark of Christian

Louboutin, whose boots average around £2,000. Swift has ten different boot styles in her tour, making the value of her clothing south of her ankles alone likely in excess of £20,000.

We have custom bodysuits by Roberto Cavalli and Versace, couture ballgowns by Ellie Saab and whimsical dresses by Italian luxury designer Alberta Ferretti – full credit to @taylorswiftstyled for these insights. That sage-green dress we mentioned? It's a custom gown, likely worth more than £5,000. Of course, Swift looks a million dollars in every single tour outfit – the effect well worth the budget spent.

Beyoncé's most recent Renaissance tour presents a similar roster of high-designer custom wear, putting behind her the days of a custom hoodie and bootie shorts (her Coachella set of two rotations of one outfit – pink and yellow – now seems modest). While these global superstars have always worn expensive, bespoke garments to perform in, never has it been so closely documented, and this enables fans to experience the shows like never before. We are closing the gap between what we understand our starlets to be capable of and also how we expect them to keep visually stimulating us, even if we're not at the show.

Of course, the artists are just part of the story. The fans are reinventing the tour experience as well – both in terms of fashion, as we have already observed, but also in terms of creativity, viral moments and community bonding.

So, make the friendship bracelets

The US leg of the Eras Tour ran from March to August 2023 – a staggering fifty-three dates marking the longest tour Swift has embarked on yet, racking up over 150 hours of singing, strutting and crowd work.

At the start of the tour, the content was an unknown quantity, with fan conversations already running high, considering the setlist, the staging and more. A post on Taylor's Instagram the week before the show launched seemed to inspire the beginning of a major online trend: a photo of her nails, painted a different colour for each Era, each album of her career, kickstarted a fanwave of content dedicated to dressing up for the tour and showcasing your allegiance to one particular album, or (of course) Era.

American fans have had the opportunity to shape what it means to be an attendee at the Eras Tour, and their influence has defined how the rest of the globe celebrates this epic event. Those who share the experience on social media have, as a result, transformed the shows into a veritable *Rocky Horror Show*, with self-created crowd participation including chants and song bolt-ons to learn, as well as outfit ideas, make-up looks and more.

There are elements of the tour that are going viral every

day. One of the most heartening demonstrations of fandom shows just how unifying being a fan can be: friendship bracelets. This is a ritual that could only have been created by the warm-hearted, high-expressionable American crowds, and a beautiful expression it is too.

Midnights features the much-beloved track five song, 'You're On Your Own, Kid', in which Swift recounts her personal journey, her younger years up to now, with both whimsy and regret – her usual sharp lyrics pass observation without judgment on the hardships she has experienced to get where she is now. As part of this song she declares, '*So make the friendship bracelets*', encouraging us as listeners and fans to seize our moments and enjoy life for the diversity of it, including the pain.

Fans have taken this expression of nostalgia and symbol of love and created something wonderful. It has led to a beautiful demonstration of generosity between fans at the shows – with (at first) the most dedicated arriving with ziplock bags full of homemade friendship bracelets beaded to match albums and Eras with song titles, lyrics and key phrases from the Taylor Swift back catalogue. By now, it is embraced by most in attendance as a way to break the ice, make friends or simply do something kind.

Fans on TikTok show arms piled high with dozens of bracelets, making conversations and friends with their fellow fans by exchanging their offerings. Friendships bracelets are more generally associated with our younger years, pre-adolescence, and offer a personal nostalgia while also slotting perfectly into the resurgence of the '90s trend, back when beaded jewellery was also in high demand.

The friendship bracelets demonstrate the power of fandom: a world where the bond and dedication to the music and the culture go beyond the artist into a community-led activity.

You don't have to look far online to find heartwarming scenes around these bracelets – one clip shows a little girl no older than seven in a warm exchange with an onsite security guard as she spends several minutes considering which of his bracelets, presumably also gifted by fans, is the right one for her. The security guard is encouraging, patient and evidently touched by the moment, probably not expecting to receive and give out meaningful accessories on his shift that night.

In other videos, high-profile celebrities are spotted in the VIP tent. In some they can be seen delighted to swap bracelets with regular punters – Ben Stiller, A-list comedic actor, appears in a video, suddenly not just Hollywood megastar but regular guy excited to see which beaded lyric will mean the most to the fans around him, taking bracelets gleefully from over the barrier he's standing behind.

Similarly, a positive narrative around Eras Tour outfit choices has flooded online platforms. A trending sound on TikTok seemed to start this highly documented activity: Taylor's voice (actually an AI production) proclaims, 'Your Eras Tour outfit looks so fucking good' paired with the chorus of 'Karma'. The sound has been used tens of thousands of times, paired with videos of fans showcasing their looks, inspired by Swift's multiple reinventions, ranging from homemade to off-the-rack inventions. We see fans barefaced, in their pyjamas, together or alone, before their final look is revealed.

The variety of looks, body types, friendship groups and budgets, paired with the endless cheerleading and acceptance in the comments sections, is amazing. There is no aspiration to do anything other than be dedicated to Taylor, to demonstrate love and loyalty for your favourite album, track or moment. It is known that Swift has declared that there is no room in her fandom for infighting (despite the hierarchy we know exists) – the Eras Tour and the celebrations around it demonstrates that. It has, at least for now, put a lot of the tension to one side and simply allowed the fanbase to celebrate their idol. We're also celebrating more than that: we're celebrating ourselves, and each other; our community that only exists because fans want to unite, because fandom is so special.

With the Eras Tour going global – with tour dates across Europe, Asia, Australia and New Zealand making this Swift's biggest undertaking ever – it is possible that the celebration of her entire career in one show, several months and millions of views has helped to solidify her position as one of the most trusted celebrities in circulation today. Fans follow Taylor's lead – this is where her power lies – but having an outlet to unify the fanbase for the first time in years, watched over by Swift herself, appears to have only built on the love and dedication she receives in return.

At the end of *Miss Americana*, Swift concludes her feelings about Eras by stating that a celebrity must, 'Live out a narrative that we [the audience] find to be interesting enough to entertain us, but not so crazy that it makes us uncomfortable. This is probably one of my last opportunities to grasp onto that kind of success, so, I dunno . . . like, as I'm reaching thirty, I'm like – I want to work really hard while society is still tolerating me being successful.'

Society indeed continues to tolerate, adulate and celebrate Taylor Alison Swift. Swift has come along way since *Miss*

'We're celebrating ourselves, and each other; our community that only exists because fans want to unite, because fandom is so SPECIAL.'

Americana, and I hope that the huge expression of love and support around the Eras Tour has helped her to tackle some of those insecurities and fears that she will not be accepted as she is.

The remembering of Taylor Swift the starlet, and her many Eras, has, perhaps, led to a personal reinvention. This show, this demonstration that marks her decade-long career, the many faces of one woman who is loved by so many, is more than just a capitalist proposition – it's proof that

we, the fans, need every version of her artistry. I think Taylor may have needed it too.

We will choose, time and time again, to celebrate Taylor Swift on this scale. As a fandom, we aspire to always affirm her career choices, to embrace her artist offerings and to follow where she will go. Sure, it was hard to get Eras Tour tickets. But it's all part of the journey we go on as fans, and it embodies our dedication to support Taylor through any endeavour.

CHAPTER 19

BLANK SPACE

The Future of Fandom

As an artist, or indeed anyone in the public eye, following on from a history-making event is undoubtedly a challenge. How does one plan their next mark on the world when their current is so monumentally game-changing as to break every record, literally improve the economy and change the face of fan culture as we know it? There are so many marks that the Eras Tour has made, both on society and on the fanbase, that all eyes are now firmly on Taylor Swift.

Indeed, it seems that celebrating Swift's past has left a gap wide open for the future – both in terms of her own career and industry, and also for fandom.

Fandom today is unique already, a product of how our society has developed and how smartphones have taken the key role of connection. Gone are the days when fans were relegated to the sidelines as screaming and hysterical, deemed unable to have clear heads when it came to their idols, be those idols men from Liverpool or teenage boys from reality television. No, fanbases today are becoming a collaboration between artist and audience –

what it means to be Taylor Swift, and what it means to be a Taylor Swift fan, is something that exists in partnership.

I'm not talking about or asking for fan unions – we don't need to have an official handshake to steer the course of the next steps taken by influencers and artists. In many ways, these unions already exist, an invisible string between us and Taylor.

When we look at the number of crazy things that have happened in just the last five years – the pandemic defined a huge number of lives and identities, withholding the experience of growing up in the real world with friends, embarrassing moments and questionable life choices – it's no wonder young people are looking for something to admire and aspire to. All these experiences used to define what it means to grow up, to shed the first light on who you might become. But in the eyes of Gen-Z, where our friends are as close to us, at least technologically, as our stars and idols, life online have never mattered more. Seeking solace and community in fandoms used to be something that happened to the most obsessed of us – the keen internet sleuths seeking similar minds – but now it's well within all our reach, ready for us to enter if we choose to walk through the virtual door.

In a world where we live online as much as we live offline, we are looking to social media and the talent that is most present and available on it to help carve out our identities, as we celebrate their personas and buy (literally) into their brands.

Is that a bad thing? This will undoubtedly be the next question everybody asks as fandom trickles out into the mainstream and we ask what the implications are for people, or more specifically, *young* people. There are many articles, books and investigations into the impact that social media has already had on our lives, but fandom and fan culture is something only really examined in academic circles or whispered about proudly by those at the source.

In the last twelve months, the word 'parasocial' has started turning up more and more in articles alongside pop culture thinkpieces about the famous and aspirational and their fangirls. Taylor Swift is in the media non-stop – anything she does is documented – whether that be fan theories and hints from the blind items, the winking eyes of the internet, or BBC News reporting on how hard it is to get Eras Tour tickets. This coverage simply did not exist a year ago, but now that fans have free rein to express just how much they love our closely held friend Taylor, everyone else is starting to catch up.

There are articles in *Cosmopolitan* about Camp Gaylore, a regular thinkpiece on Refinery29 about fan phenomena, interviews asking celebrities directly about their fan culture online. So if they're getting up to speed on our world, what else could change?

I want to focus on the positives – if parasocial relationships are heightening our closeness to, and therefore how influenced we are by, stars like Taylor and Harry, what kind of influence are they having on younger generations? And I don't just mean music tastes – I think it goes so much deeper than that.

I think we are already seeing the changes. Olivia Rodrigo, the twenty-year-old singer-songwriter from California we looked at in Chapter 6, started her young budding career as a Disney actress and performer. Olivia has, just outside of her teen years, achieved almost instant fame with a left-turn to solo artistry. Her debut album, *Sour,* is a thoughtful, raw pop record that describes in brutal detail the experience of breaking up with your first love. To be more specific, Olivia tells us, the listener, the details of *her* break up with *her* first love. It is, obviously, a great album. Her soul searching, sadness sharing, sobering sourness – perhaps none of it would exist without the path being laid by Taylor Swift for more music that is open, honest and *authentic*.

Is Taylor Swift teaching us all how to be more real?

Disappearing are the days when the qualms of teenage life, young adult emotion, didn't matter to anybody, creating a loneliness so palpable and memorable that I still get shivers recalling it.

Our teen spirit, our misery and intense feels are no longer an isolating experience – they're a call to arms.

We have the likes of Sabrina Carpenter, Maisie Peters and mega-famous Billie Eilish all opening their hearts as we open our wallets – sharing their musical talent with us in the form of their most private feelings, and we can't get enough of it. Lizzie McAlpine's 'ceilings', a modest track at face value, went unfathomably viral on TikTok. Full of romantic, innocent lyrics about young love and fantasy, Lizzie captured in three minutes what so many adults fail to understand about their own teen experiences in a lifetime – they're long forgotten by many once you're all grown up.

But younger generations now don't need adults. They have each other at every level of the food chain – it could be your friends on Snapchat who you send DMs to, or via your favourite songwriter who sees you through their lyrics.

Thanks to Taylor, thanks to social media, and thanks to the amazing young people that exist now (that's you – hi!) we are opening the door to a more vulnerable legion of viral talent, born from musicians who are still young too, trying to make sense of life. It never gets easier, really, but is it helping young people feel seen, and as such less scared to embrace life with open arms, even the bits that suck?

Respect for their young fanbases has been something that stars like Taylor have shown in abundance. Look at the wording of her post asking fans to consider voting in 2018:

> 'So many intelligent, thoughtful, self-possessed people have turned eighteen in the past two years and now have the right and privilege to make their vote count.'

This tone-setting on how to address a young audience was unique to Taylor in her years of development as a superstar – and it has created a system of mutual trust with her fans. Young adult fans can be the biggest, loudest, most passionate champions. If their artists show them love and respect, they will return it in spades.

It means they are shown their value, helped to understand that their voice matters. This could be lifechanging.

Our idols today, it seems, take us more seriously than our teachers, our parents, our lawmakers. They understand what we are going through, and it makes us *stronger*.

We live in a world where, thanks to the pandemic, young people have felt their spirits travel to the darkest of places way before they might have. Without structure and support networks, or the meaningful relationships that help teens become who they are meant to be, being a young person in the pandemic must have fucking sucked – with the most important moments stripped away. It might seem insignificant, but trips to the cinema with your besties or sneaking into parties to get a glimpse of your crush, or sitting next to your frenemy in class and doing better on your coursework than them . . . it all matters so much more than we realise. Three whole years' worth of teenagers simply didn't get to have that.

Looking for support in music, art and online platforms was more important than ever, and it wasn't just a passing trend – the floodgates are still open. I think that has the power to make our world a better place.

Therapy and mental health are talked about more freely, in media, music and daily life than they ever have been. The breadth of conversation about inclusivity broadens continuously, with shows like the incredible *Heartstopper* inviting young people to accept themselves as they are. More young people are attending protests and rallies than ever – asking for a better government, better rights and acceptance for all, for climate change to be tackled and plastic to be reduced. Greta Thunberg was fifteen years old when her activism for climate change started catching fire in the media. It is no wonder the next generation is called Alpha – these kids are getting shit done, despite their own adversities.

Are fandom, our communities and our idols helping this become the new reality?

The voices of teenagers being heard has been a long time coming, and it is at least in part thanks to the bold and brave actions of artists like Taylor Swift that we are where we are today – not just to be political superstars or using their money to support causes (though it helps), but by showing us their true selves to help us find our own.

You can't exhale today without seeing a tweet about Taylor Swift's impact (maybe that is just my supercharged algorithm, to be fair).

> # By taking fandom seriously, we give it power, and by giving it power we give it space to create change.

And when I say change, what do I mean? I mean a future with more possibility, more optimism and vulnerability. Taylor Swift changed *my* life in so many ways. She helped me to become a person who can express their feelings, who can find value and meaning in the harder moments. I grew up in a world where this was not the norm, and so it has taken me into my thirties to really see the transformation take hold, and to understand how it has changed me. I am a woman running her own business in part because of Taylor Swift. I feel secure in my opinionated, direct personality in

'Let's make the
world a better place
by opening up our
hearts and souls.

Let's do what
Taylor Swift did –
shake it off,
or try it on.'

part because of Taylor Swift. I can stand up and have the tough conversations in life without shame, and, guess what? It's because of Taylor Swift. She helped me make a path to stand by what was right for me.

If the landscape had been different, if my love had been legitimised sooner, who would I be today?

That excites me, and should excite you, the young person reading this book. Your idol is inspirational, and smart, and funny, and business-minded. Your other favourite pop stars are too. There are so many young women on the stage today who care about you and what you are going through. And you? You are in touch with your emotions, and have somebody to experience them with. As you grow up, you understand that it is cool to be ambitious. It is possible to put yourself forward as an advocate for change, or a boss babe with a talent for making cold hard cash. And while you do these things, you can experience life, and love, and understand yourself and the world around you a little bit better with every confident (or shaky, who cares?) step you take.

Let's make the world a better place by opening up our hearts and souls. Let's do what Taylor Swift did – shake it off, or try it on. Feel gorgeous, or messy, or vengeful, or mean, or romantic. And tell us about it, please, so that the generation beneath you continues to embrace this movement of making peace with our messiness. I'll be watching as you do.

CHAPTER 20

DEAR READER

Epilogue

I wanted to write this book not to analyse fandom from an outsider perspective, to unpack our world for the people who don't get it. I wrote this book for you, and for me, and for anybody who has ever been a fan of anything. Being a fan shows your capacity to open your heart, to love with your full weight, and I think that is a joyous thing that should be celebrated. As we have explored, fandom is a beautiful, crazy, intense thing. I hope I have helped you to understand it a little bit better, and perhaps to understand yourself along the way.

If I might ask you to take one thing away from this book, it is this:

honour your fandom, believe in your inner voice – but also know when you should question your perception.

It is easy, when you love a star, when you completely trust their ideology, to take everything we think we know, or hear, or learn at face value. Fandoms are communities full of hierarchy and expectation, and the world of celebrity is even messier.

We simply no longer live in a world where somebody, especially a public figure, going against the grain is private and without consequences. We want to share what we think and feel, which is important – and more than anything, we want to be sure that our perspective aligns with those who exist in the same community as us, who like the same things we like.

But I hope we have found through our journey together that there is always more than meets the eye when it comes to opinions, viewpoints and, of course, love. Fandom is a joyful thing, but it comes with heightened emotions. Those emotions can cause us to make misjudgements, or to forget about the real-life people who exist behind social media handles, or their music, or public persona.

These are the ups and downs of fandom, and indeed they reflect the ups and downs of our lives.

We humans are a pretty predictable bunch. We are easily threatened and hurt and annoyed. We also love to feel that people understand us, and that *our* tribe is on *our* side. The internet has never given us so many opportunities to bump into the tribes that trouble us, or that don't match our personal ideologies. Here's my question to you: if those people were not online, but were sitting next to you in the park, or at a friend's birthday party with you, how would you judge them then? Would you see their opinions differently, ignore them and move on?

I suppose what I'm getting at is this: there are people online who are problematic, and then there are people online who are different to you. The two things aren't the same – and I think we can make fandoms even better, more fun and inclusive, if we learn that they are made up of amazing, cool, multifaceted people with varying views.

We ask a lot of our personal idols these days: we want them to be shiny and beautiful and exciting, to perform their hearts out and to give us their souls. We ask them to tell us how we should feel about the big things in life, and the bad things in the world. We get mad if they don't – or perhaps they can't – or if their advice or position doesn't meet the expectation we had, the predictions we'd made based on our forensic understanding of them. We become disappointed and mad at them, and we lose some faith. And I think because we can't directly address our idols, we turn to each other to fight it out.

But how about this? Fandom is such a beautiful thing, as is loving something freely and shamelessly, and maybe it belongs more to you, within you, than it does outside of you, within the Taylor Swifts of the world, or within the members of our fandom who we don't fully agree with.

What if instead of asking celebrities to tell us what they think, we think more about what we're asking of them, and what that tells us about ourselves. Your path, your moral compass is inside you, and while we can learn so much from the people and celebrities we admire, be sure that you hold onto that joyful thing that makes you *you*.

Don't ever lose sight of the joyful things that make you HAPPY.

I have learned so much while writing this book. I have gone back inside myself to reignite my own fandom and it has been hugely revealing. I have examined my own shame and fear at the same time. It is vulnerable to love things, and it is challenging too. I don't really know anything more about that than when I was fifteen, apart from knowing that I love things and I love them completely. I find the most joy I can experience when I'm embracing my inner fangirl, and I feel myself gaining literal physical energy from doing so.

Some people don't, and some people don't get it, and that's okay too. We don't have to hide it anymore. How magic is that?

What I love most about all of this, and what has spurred me on when writing this book for you, for us, is how young people, how *you*, can change our world for the better. You're *already* doing it. To give voice to the hard things that we go through in our formative years, to give power to the joys and fun and madness of what excites and satisfies us when we are young is to keep it in our hearts a little longer. Hold onto it for as long as you can. Because eventually, trust me, life starts to get in the way. The real world can kind of suck sometimes, but isn't it impossibly cool that we have an outlet and communities that will always exist to help us escape for a little while?

If I have a bad day, or an anxiety flare-up, there is nothing more soothing and consoling to me than listening to Taylor Swift. She is there for me in a way that perhaps I'll never be able to tell her. But you know what? I think she knows. Taylor keeps going for many reasons – she is ambitious, and she is the most famous woman in the world right now. She is creative, and an artist, and her unstoppable force isn't going anywhere. But I also think this is what drives her: she sees how much we relate to her, and how much we need her.

She isn't just telling her own story anymore: she's helping us to tell _ours_, too.

The fact that this outlet is starting to take hold of the wider circles of the world, that people are beginning to ask what parasocial relationships are and why they matter, that people are testing out fan theories and that fans are influencing the work of their idols, is an incredible thing. I could never have imagined it when I hid in my bedroom in my teen years, writing _Harry Potter_ fanfiction and making friends in forums and falling in love with someone I'd never met, all because of fandom.

So, to close, it's only right that I borrow the words of the woman that has inspired me for over a decade and inspired this whole book:

make the friendship bracelets.
Take the moment and taste it.

By doing what you're doing right now, by choosing to love something and share that love with the world, you *are* making it a better place.

And for that I say thank you, from the bottom of my perfectly good heart. You're not on your own, kid. There are so many of us who feel just like you. And that, that, right there, is the magic of fandom.

ACKNOWLEDGEMENTS

LOOK WHAT YOU MADE ME DO

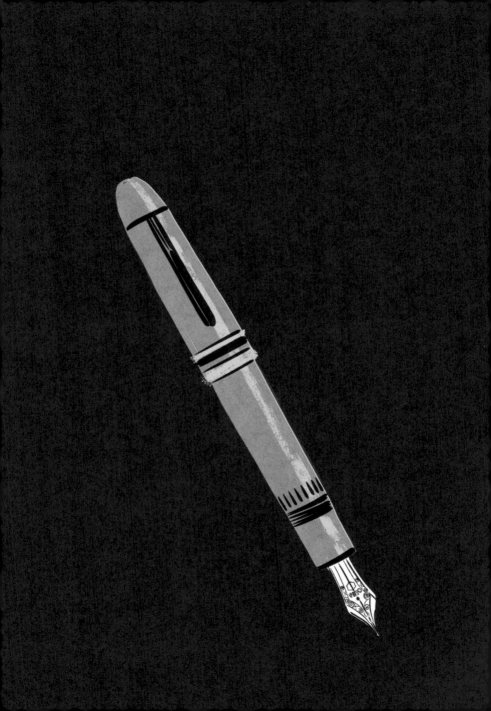

It's me, hi! Having worked in publishing for a few years, I know all too well that a book cannot happen with just one person, so I have some people to thank. Firstly, thank you to the team of people who came together to turn a blank space into a book:

My agent, Chloe Seager, who instantly understood this book and whose calm confidence in me has kept me going. Thank you for being fearless, and for taking my hand and dragging me headfirst through the mad publishing journey. I would totally dance with you in a storm in my best dress.

My editor, Yas Morrissey, was the first person who told me I could write – thank you for that, first and foremost. Your enthusiasm and expertise have guided me through this process. Thank you for ensuring that my voice was always part of this project and for being a brilliant collaborator.

Thank you to everyone at Simon & Schuster Children's Books. S&S gave me my first job at a publishing house, so it means a lot that it is now my first publishing home. Rachel Denwood and Laura Hough, thank you for totally getting the vision and brimming with enthusiasm, as well as huge ambition, energy, and strategic planning. There is no pair of powerhouses I would trust more to publish me. Dani Wilson, you're a gem. I'm incredibly lucky that you are part of the team bringing this book to market. Olivia Horrox and Ellen Abernethy, thank you for your marketing and publicity expertise. I couldn't have asked for a more talented pair to share this book with our fellow Swifties. Sean Williams, thank you for making this book look gorgeous (I can't say anything to its face!). Thanks to anyone in the team who had a hand in making this book happen. I'm so grateful for all your hard work.

Thank you to the creators who spoke to me when I was researching this book: Shannon McNamara, Steven Sullivan, Ashley Hamilton, Claire Parker, Alexandra Wormley, Dave Fawbert from Swiftogeddon, and DeuxMoi. I'm so appreciative of your time and insight.

There are a handful of people who I would not have considered writing this book without their early enthusiasm:

Georgia Henry, who told me that I could make anybody want to read anything. It was probably the wine talking, but it meant more than you know. Bethany Rutter, for being such an inspiring friend who has shown me that no aspiration is too big, and for many chats about writing (and life) over countless fun dates. Sarah Plows, you were the first to listen to a – rough and ready – idea over gelato. Thank you for telling me you wanted to read *that* book. Jane Griffiths, thank you for seeing the seeds of promise early on. Sabina, thank you, simply, for being you.

Holly Bourne: my gratitude for your constant support is beyond words (but I have to write something here . . .). I owe you a huge debt for all the excitement, enthusiasm and time you have given to this book, as well as my journey as an author. Your advice and friendship have been incomparable. Thank you so, so much. I've made a friend for life.

Thank you to the dear friends who have been such an important part of my publishing journey: Nina, Paul, Bea, Lucy, Stephie, Katie, Lizz, Katherine, Rosi, Lauren, Harriet, Claire, Emma. I came into this industry for the books . . . but I stayed for the friends I made along the way. I appreciate each one of you.

There are so many authors, illustrators and colleagues that have given me advice, support, inspiration and friendship over the years. I am lucky to know you all. Thank you.

I am fortunate to have some friends who are practically family: Siobhan, what would I do without you? You're the kind of friend people dream to have in their life. Nicola, thank you for reminding me that I'm living my dream, and for being an amazing friend for thirty years. Carla – my oldest pally, and thank the heavens!!! I'm grateful to each of you for being there before, during, and after the pages of this book.

Thank you from the bottom of my heart to my *actual* family: Andy, Emma and Toby, your constant support means so much to me. Dad and Blin, thank you for teaching me that hard work always pays off. Keith, we wouldn't be a complete family without you (now imagine I'm saying something sarcastic to take the edge off).

And, for Mum: I wouldn't love books and stories if it weren't for you. I wouldn't be a writer if it weren't for you.

I wouldn't have known a deep love of words without your lifelong enthusiasm for them. Thank you for everything you do and for making me laugh like nobody else does.

I simply don't think this book would exist if it weren't for my sweet angels Ruby and Taylor. They're cats, so they can't read this, but they are the ones that finally gave me peace.

Growing up, I was painfully shy. I owe a gratitude to every person I encountered in fandoms as a teenager who helped me to see that I could make real friends. Thank you to Callie, my first writing partner. You believed in me before many others did.

Finally: I must extend such gratitude to the woman who inspired this book: Taylor Swift. For every time that my life has known darkness, your music was a light. For every time I didn't have words to articulate how I was feeling, your lyrics somehow did. For the times over the years when I was happy, free, confused and lonely at the same time, your songwriting and spirit have been a source of fun, hope and joy. Thank you for showing me you can be a woman with ambition and imperfections, and still make the whole place shimmer. I wrote a book because of you . . . literally, look what you made me do.